CONCI

CONCILIUM 2007/1

# PLURALIST THEOLOGY:
# THE EMERGING PARADIGM

Edited by

Luiz Carlos Susin

Andrés Torres Queiruga

José María Vigil

*with the collaboration of the*
*Latin American Theological Commission of EATWOT*

SCM Press · London

Published by SCM Press, 9–17 St Albans Place, London N1 0NX

ISBN 978 0 334 03092 8

Printed and bound in Great Britain by
William Clowes Ltd, Beccles, Suffolk

*Concilium* published February, April, June, October
December

# Contents

# Introduction: Emergence and Urgency of the New Pluralist Paradigm

LUIZ CARLOS SUSIN

*Concilium* is a review in the Catholic tradition, conciliar in tone, with an ecumenical spirit. The 'signs of the times' demand daring in examining and elaborating new depths of 'catholicity' and of the spirit of ecumenism. The increasingly obvious emergence of pluralism, to the point where it marks a new paradigm, compels a new and more forceful approach to it, seeking new insights and trying out a new language. ASETT, the Latin American Theological Commission of EATWOT (Ecumenical Association of Third World Theologians) proposed a jointly-edited issue of *Concilium*, in which Latin American theology would draw into its tradition what theology produced in the Anglo-Saxon context had been developing in a somewhat different form: a theology that, rather than being one 'of religious pluralism', is a pluralist theology, elaborated on the basis of a *pluralist paradigm*, and one that is, effectively, a *liberating* pluralist theology, based on the approach of the option for the poor. The challenge had, in fact, been clearly issued to liberation theology by Aloysius Pieris, on the grounds that religious pluralism has everything to do with the multitudes of poor people, as is confirmed here in the article by José María Vigil. Following a series of publications by ASETT,[1] this issue of the review, as a partnership between ASETT and *Concilium*, displays not only world-wide collaboration, as is necessary today, but also a fruitful marriage between liberation theology and theology of pluralism, showing that liberation theology has not remained stuck in the themes of past decades but is tackling new concerns, such as this *pluralist liberation theology*.

The 'plural condition' as a mark of our time, difference and diversity, 'pluralism' developing as an interpretative concept: is all this a historical novelty or simply a fact of life that has always been there, but of which we now have a new understanding fraught with consequences? The argument of this issue of *Concilium* is that pluralism is a paradigm imposed in place of

7

the uniqueness, universalism, and 'absolutism' of traditional thought, of metaphysics, and – even more so – of a western outlook. Pluralism is a matter of understanding the complexity of the deeper reality of life in all its aspects, including social, cultural, and religious. The complexity of reality in its plural condition calls for and requires discernment. It requires a 'new awakening', which is now an awakening from the *dogmatic religious dream*, and a 'new enlightenment', of religious stamp, based on otherness and plurality, instead of on subjectivity and an identity with claims to exclusive universality and absolute uniqueness. It also requires a bold acceptance of the epistemological change, with all this implies, which is taking place, irrevocably, in our time.

Certain questions guided the editors of this issue of *Concilium*: Could religious pluralism be just a consequence of the course taken by Christianity in the phase of modernity; that is, a western phenomenon that does not concern other religious traditions? Or are all religions called to make this paradigmatic leap? And what resources would they have for doing so? Are elements of universality and acceptance of pluralism as a form of this universality not to be found already in different religious traditions?

Faced with the pluralism and complexity of our age, contemporary societies are either exasperating each other by insisting on affirming their identities in religious fundamentalist accents or splitting into fragments with no unifying religious horizons. But these confrontations in religious terms are bound up with a more inclusive and perhaps more urgent reality than the religions themselves: divisive market-based globalization, which is creating a new, globalized form of *apartheid*, threatening the future of the poor masses and that of all forms of life on earth. Globalization can bring positive values, such as encouragement of democracy and human rights. Seen from the vast regions where the people are ever more excluded from its benefits, however, it forces peoples who feel its malevolent effects to seek ways of resisting in their humanity through recourse to the deepest sources of their religious roots. Religious pluralism can, then, appear ambiguous: on the one hand, it can be the fruit of fundamentalist resistance and even of violence in affirming one's own identity; on the other, it can be a legitimate and civilized expression of cultural identity, of its religious root, of its 'soul' with its right to be different within human bio–diversity, resisting the over-whelming power of claims to universality based on the privilege of being the most powerful. Our arguments here stress this positive reality in under-standing religious pluralism, seeing it in the light of a creating, revealing, and saving plan, a manifestation of the unfathomable divinity in the plurality of life on earth. And they seek to deconstruct the remains of inclusivist and unifying claims based on a privileged centre. Evidently, as will be seen, this spells trouble for Christian thinking.

Religious and ecclesiastical institutions are hesitant about embarking on the route to accepting religious pluralism as a sign of the times and of the living God, of respect for cultural and religious bio-diversity, of hospitality, and of life's riches. The difficulty is understandable, particularly for religions with claims to universality. We do not yet know how to react positively to pluralism in terms of mission, of ecumenism, of inter-religious hospitality, of acceptance of the cultural bio-diversity in which religions can express themselves with deeper human riches and provide an encounter with the divine.

What is nevertheless certain is that religious pluralism, apart from being a fact of life now, and one that has come to stay, will also become more extensive and more complex. What cost in sacrifice and violence will this acceleration in complexity entail? What can we learn in time? Shall we learn to see soon enough, with discernment, greeting religious pluralism as divine creation and taking a coherent approach to it?

As Christians, we know that one of the great challenges posed by religious pluralism is how to understand the universality of revelation and salvation in Jesus and, at the same time, without half measures, the revelatory or salvific value – including universal value – of other religions. Most of us would go down the path of 'inclusivism', saying, for example, that there is something of the grace of Christ or the universality of the breath of the Spirit in a good Buddhist. But how would we react if a Buddhist told us there is something of Buddha's enlightenment in a good Christian? Can we take the others' inclusivism as seriously as our own? In other words, is it worth carrying on with inclusivism?

On the other hand, pluralism cannot be grasped in the abstract, passing over the real and even radical differences among religions. This would be an unrepentant universalism of sublimation via abstraction of our particular characteristics. It dissimulates the will to power, colonization, the reducing of others. The West knows all this well, and it deserves all the criticism it gets. Pluralism, as a thought-paradigm and an attitude fully adopted, obliges us to abandon any pretension to absolute and panoramic ways, to unilateral exclusions or inclusions.

To adopt a tranquil 'henotheism', however, comfortable with accepting that each nation and each culture has its own god, while tolerance and indifference among religions goes on in the same old way, would be a return

to an archaic attitude that does not match up to the complexity of relationships in our world today. Indifference, in a world where those different from
us are ever closer to us, turns out to be a subtle form of violence. In today's
West, marked by fragmentation of individualities, the new religious experiences tend to produce new syntheses or syncretisms out of diverse sources
and traditions. Could these be 'moving beyond' pluralism, or are they just
individual and fragile defences against the gale of globalization, one of the
forms of indifference?

In their institutional aspect, religions today, together with all major
institutions, are undergoing changes increasingly seen to be global. The
sensation is of loss of power and of proving inadequate. A 'liquid' spirituality
(to use a term coined by Zygmunt Bauman) contained within walls that
are becoming increasingly porous and permeable, with increasing open
breaches, is one of the signs of the times. Will a spirituality without religion
become possible, or will spirituality create new forms of religion, albeit now
within a pluralist paradigm? The fact is that pluralism needs a corresponding spirituality.

Readers can add many questions of their own to these. This issue of
*Concilium* cannot claim either to exhaust the questions or to give fully
worked-out answers to them. Its claim is to something more urgent for the
present: to carry out some analyses, to develop some indications, to set some
tasks in train, and to make some attempts. This is not a little: it is bringing
to birth, in pain and affliction, essaying new categories, trying out some
neologisms. New realities need a new language, with all its attendant risks
and burdens, beginning with misunderstandings. Our contributors are not
lacking in good cheer, alongside the seriousness with which each seeks to
articulate tradition with the novelty and promise that are emerging in this
new paradigm.

We begin (Part I) with the most global aspect of our common home, the
earth, with our human family. The harsh reality of centuries of history and
of western hegemony has brought us to a new and unprecedented level of
*apartheid* and to a cul-de-sac for the earth and its children. It is Mother Earth
herself and the life of the poor that are calling for a radical break. And the
possibility of a future can only come from a massive mutual learning process,
from dialogue, from hospitality, and from common endeavours using our
plurality of resources. The pluralist paradigm is not a requirement for
Christianity alone. It is a vital need, one that permeates and challenges
cultures, peoples, all traditions and forms of religion.

Part II consists of theological considerations that take stock of cultures, traditions, and languages. Our main support comes from the general idea of discernment: first to provide a favourable interpretation of the *kairós*, the opportune moment, the signs that show theology what to think about, what to investigate, what to debate. How do we approach revelation in the plurality of revelations, of languages, of cultural symbols? How do we combine universality and real particularity in religious experience? How do we understand the specific 'form' of Jesus, the Christ and Son of God according to Christian belief, against a pluralist horizon? Even if the living reality of faith communities is more important than the epistemology required to describe their experiences correctly, nevertheless epistemology and fresh language are requirements of our human condition. We have to risk losing and being open to new images and concepts. Thinking in generational terms, faced with young people who embody the shape of pluralism, perhaps we need to be more radical than providing new bottles for new wine and develop new wine for new bottles, as one contributor says.

In Part III we deal with some practical consequences for missionary approach, for spirituality, for religion as such. Seeing the world, our common home, with God's eyes, at this time of religions coming closer together, as are all other human dimensions, brings consequences. Whether they are to be a fruitful blessing or a threat of chaos depends largely on our decision and our response.

We dedicate this issue of *Concilium* to the memory of Jacques Dupuis. Matthew's Gospel begins appreciation of the 'religion of others', with the surprising visit of three wise men from the East, brought about by their seeing, there in the East, a great star shining, a religious sign banished from biblical orthodoxy. Our age and our theology have come to know other wise men from the East: Raymund Panikkar, Aloysius Pieris, Tissa Balasuriya, these three followed by Michael Amaladoss, Felix Wilfred (currently president of the Editorial Board of this review), and others. Jacques Dupuis began by following the opposite path, the path of the missionaries who set out from the West for the continents of the East and South. Many of them experienced the physical shock of the difference and of what Jon Sobrino (also on our Editorial Board) has called the epistemological break, not so much as a theoretical approach and work programme but rather as the result of an *aporia* – scandal and madness – and of a respectful apophatism toward divine transcendence in the experience of God together with others, received as a grace by means of others. The continents of Asia, Africa, and Latin America are witnesses to this transformation of innumerable missionaries into spokespersons for a new theological *locus*, strengthened in their suffering by this conviction that revelation and salvation are truly grace because they break the logic of religion, make us understand and stammer that 'what is within is there outside; the height is there below, the blessing is together with the cursed, the judgment on the world is first pronounced by the littlest ones'. Jacques Dupuis returned to Rome, to the centre, insisting that the new paradigm no longer has a centre. His Christian theology of religious pluralism is coherent with the steps of an about-turn, which demanded a 'decentralization'. In his Trinitarian theology of religious pluralism, therefore, the Holy Spirit is God's kiss for the entire world, the catholicity that includes the world and its pluriform religious life.

Jacques Dupuis became an Abrahamic wise man, a master who took steps and opened paths, uniting his studies with his experience. He died under suspicion from those who know others only from within their studies. Nevertheless, 'what must be has power', and his companions and disciples carry on, taking fresh strides forward. This issue of *Concilium*, produced in collaboration with the Latin American Theological Commission of the Ecumenical Association of Third World Theologians, pays homage to a colleague and a master. And, in his honour, it essays new steps in faithfulness to the same Spirit that breathes with freedom and life.

The editors wish to thank Virgil Elizondo, Edward Farrugia, Claude Geffré, Rosino Gibellini, Maureen Junker-Kenny, and Marie-Theres Wacker for their assistance.

*Translated by Paul Burns*

## Note

1. Cf. the series, 'Por los muchos caminos de Dios' (Down God's many paths), 5 vols, Quito: Abya Yala, 2002–7. Available at http://www.latinoamericana.org/tiempoaxial. Published in Spanish, Portuguese, and Italian.

# I. The Situation

# The Religions – mainly Christianity – Facing the Future

TISSA BALASURIYA, OMI

In this essay I wish to deal with two basic factors that are not generally taken into adequate account concerning the issues relating to the life of the poor, the life of the earth, and the future of religions. The first is the origin and nature of the present world system that has come into being mainly since 1492, and the second is its link to the long prevalent classical Christian theological paradigm. They are inter-connected. The alliance between western powers and the Church(es) helped these nations in their quest for wealth and power through colonial expansion, and on the other hand the Churches were helped to develop a theology that contributed to the power of the Christian rulers and peoples. These two factors are of deeper and longer-term significance than the recent process of globalization and the present-day general discussion on inter-religious relations.

Correspondingly, the remedying of the unjust world system requires radical changes in the world structure, far beyond present approaches of countries or peoples' movements; and the remedying of Christian theology demands a radical reorientation of Christian thought and action if it is to be in keeping with genuine discipleship of Jesus Christ. Both these are basic and foundational changes in the world order and in Christian life and thought. What follows is a brief presentation, given the limit of space, leaving readers to fill in the data implied in the argument.

## I. The World System

In the world today more than one out of four persons are poor and lack the bare minimum required for a healthy and dignified human existence. The relative differences in the standards of living and wealth of peoples is greater than ever before in human history. Five hundred years ago, at the end of the fifteenth century, while the indigenous peoples of the Americas and of Oceania were at a lower stage of technological advancement, there was a greater similarity in the standards of living of peoples of the other continents, Eurasia and Africa, which were related to each other through trade links.

The history of the world shows that while the peoples of Europe, especially the elite, grew in wealth and power the vast majority of the peoples of the rest of the world remained at a substantially lower standard of living. The development from a primitive agricultural economy to an industrial economy came about first in the more enterprising European countries. Expanding European powers such as Britain, France, Holland, Belgium, Russia, Germany, and Italy colonized much of the rest of the world. The resources of the colonized peoples, including land, technology, and skills were exploited for the economic development of the colonizers; who by the use of political and military power also determined the conditions of trade. Exports from the colonies were on terms set by the markets of the colonizers, and colonial economies were made dependent.

Thus Sri Lanka produced tea for British companies and markets. Good agricultural lands were converted to tea estates; indentured labour from South India was brought to serve in semi-slave-like conditions on tea and rubber plantations owned by the British. As a result the ethnic mix of the population was substantially altered, to the extent of contributing to future ethnic problems in the country.

While services in colonies, such as education and health, benefited from the cultural and technological changes, the economy became subservient to the interests of the rulers. The European powers grew in wealth and resources at an unprecedented rate, while the colonies stagnated relatively, even absolutely. At the same time a collaborative elite class emerged among the colonized. This system prevailed worldwide till the end of the Second World War in 1945.

After independence, in the 1940s, 1950s, and 1960s, the former colonized peoples set out to fashion a society to suit their own needs and to achieve self-reliant economic growth. East Asian countries succeeded partially, with

China and India becoming major world economies in the 1990s. Most former colonies, however, remain dependent on foreign investment and on foreign export markets. In the new global system the world map has been redrawn to suit the priorities of the victors, especially in relation to ownership of land, distribution of population, and world trade. The European Union has ensured relative peace in Europe for sixty years since 1945, together with substantial technological and economic growth. After the collapse of the USSR in 1989 the USA has emerged as the sole global superpower.

In the new world order, under the nominal world leadership of the United Nations Organization (UNO), former colonial powers have kept their privileged positions. The UNO is largely controlled by the former western colonial powers. Their privileged position in the Security Council gives the five major powers who were victors in WW II the right of veto. The rich western powers use their economic and political power in agencies such as the International Monetary Fund (IMF), the World Bank, and now the World Trade Organization (WTO).

The global dominance of the western powers within the world system is the product of expansion and domination by the European nations in the five hundred years since 1492. The land distribution among peoples remains substantially the same as in 1945, after five centuries of European colonial expansion since 1492. Now a system of neo-liberal colonialism has been set in place partly under the aegis of the UNO and its agencies.

As the statistics indicate, during the second half of the twentieth century there were significant changes in the relative population of the western countries and of the rest of the world. Thus countries such as China and India have limited land despite a very high population.

## II. World Apartheid

The European peoples have taken over much of the available arable land of the earth in the least populated areas such as the Americas, Russia, and Oceania. They claim these lands on the basis of conquest, or first occupation (*primi occupantis*). They restrict immigration to these lands on the basis of race, wealth, or technical skills and sometimes admit cheap labour for dirty, dangerous, and difficult jobs. At present the Whites are insufficient in numbers to populate them but are unwilling to share their ill-gotten property with needy poorer families of different racial stock.

Without a just and peaceful remedy for this imbalance there will be no guarantee of life and security for the billions who are poor, nor will the rich countries be able to prevent an overflow of population from the South to their under-cultivated areas. Capitalist globalization not only fails to provide solutions for this problem but makes the situation worse by the policies of structural adjustment of the IMF and the WTO. Neither is the UNO, as it is presently conceived and structured, capable of finding meaningful solutions for this imbalance.

## III. Foundational injustice of the killer world system

This imbalance of population to land is in a sense the foundational injustice of the whole world system today, inherited from the colonial period. Its preservation is thought of as the maintenance of peace and law in the world. This may be called global apartheid and is one of the biggest structural evils that continue from generation to generation. Some of its characteristics are:

(a) It is a result of violence and land grab, consolidated by the victors in terms of territorial frontiers and carried on from generation to generation. It is based on 'might is right';

(b) it is racism of an extreme form; it also leads to the fear of the disadvantaged races by the possessors of land and hence to defensive militarism;

(c) it is the most basic form of inequality and deprivation, from which others, such as of incomes, wealth, and resources flow;

(d) it deprives people in need of the opportunities of work, food, and livelihood;

(e) the unfair terms of trade and the burden of foreign debt weigh most heavily on the poor;

(f) it helps increase land, water, and air pollution; it leads to waste of resources by neglect, by non-cultivation, and perhaps by over-fertilization;

(g) it is against the principle of 'the free market' for the freedom of movement of persons; it is maintained by unjust immigration laws, leads to illegal immigration and refugees. It is a basic cause of social conflicts in and among countries, and it contributes to expenditure on arms; it is a centennial form of injustice for which no adequate solution is in sight, it makes people insensitive to the needs of others and to the evils of the past consequent on former violence;

(h) it goes against the core values of the religions, which advocate that the whole earth should be available to all humankind and teach sharing to be a principal virtue;

(i) it affects Latin American countries in issues such as employment and migration. But it also helps them in so far as the Latin American countries and peoples are also the post-colonial land owners and beneficiaries of the world system.

This problem is neglected by most economists, political scientists, politicians, planners, international lawyers, and theologians. It is not generally studied by universities and international foundations. It is not within the scope of the religions, especially Christianity. Since the demographic data indicate a worsening situation in the course of the twenty-first century, it is a challenge for the young people of today to participate in making the world more just by bringing about changes in mindsets as well as global structures of the world system. Most solutions for development, justice, and peace at present under discussion are piecemeal and reformist, keeping the unjust foundational system intact. It may be called *the original sin of the western world*.

The peoples of the South are increasing in numbers, younger in age, and in several countries acutely short of land for cultivation. The frustration of young people reaches revolutionary levels when they see the fate of their countries as a result of the world socio-economic system and the selfishness of the rich countries and their own ruling elites, who neglect the needs of the poor. Already the push from the South is bringing in migrants and refugees to the more prosperous and peaceful North. This corresponds to a pull from the countries of the North, which have an ageing and relatively declining population and invite foreign workers when they need labour. The affluent North seems to encourage policies of extermination of the poor in the South by internal wars, famine, birth prevention, and other ways to economic and population management. The present world order leaves little room for justice to the peoples of the South.

Many realize that *this economic and social order is unsustainable*, owing to the destruction of nature and exhaustion of non-renewable resources. It is against the future of humanity and of succeeding generations. The impact of climate change and of pollution of the earth is hardest on the poor peoples of the South and East.

The prevailing world system is more insidious in many senses than the colonial period. It is seductive in its oppression of the poorer and weaker sections of all countries. It incorporates the elites of most countries to maintain its acceptance. It is shown and seen as inevitable: 'There is no alternative'.

In these perspectives the entire rhetoric of world justice, human rights, peace, debt payment, and aid has to be rethought. There has to be a deconstruction of the dialogue on development, human rights, and international law and justice. But since the rich powers and their academia and media condition the cultural framework of thinking on such issues, the just interests of the poor are not taken into account in the discussion and decisions among the rich – as at the summit conferences of the G8. They are not highlighted even in the discourse among the governments of the poor peoples as in the Non-Aligned Movement. Even Churches and people's organizations do not deal seriously with this global apartheid. Much of the discussion and planning concerning economic and political development takes the existing world system for granted and implicitly assumes it to be legitimate.

My approach to global ethics would be that this world system is basically unjust and is the fruit of the greatest exploitation of other peoples and the earth's resources in history, mainly by peoples of European origin. It is the result of violence, robbery, colossal land grab, and the greatest genocide in human history. Yet this reality is not taken into account in prevailing international law. Thus national sovereignty for the existing powers is taken for granted.

## IV. Christianity and the world system

How did the establishment of this colonial system impact religions? Prior to 1492 religions were limited mainly to their continental homes of origin. Christians were mostly in Europe and the Middle East, Hindus in India, Muslims and Jews in the Middle East, Muslims in Africa and parts of Asia, Confucianism in China, Shintoism in Japan, and the natural religions and indigenous peoples' religions almost everywhere. There was a correlation between the land and the religions, with population movements gradually changing the geographical areas of religions, as with the spread of Buddhism in Asia.

After 1492 there was a very significant shift in the world distribution of population defined by religion. Christianity spread to the Americas and to Oceania as the dominant faith and was taken to the African and Asian countries by western missioners working with the colonial powers. A map of the world distribution of religions shows that most of the post-1492 'new world' regions have become habitations of Christians of different denominations.

How was the *teaching of Jesus*, that his disciples should love God and their neighbour as themselves, interpreted in this period of colonial expansion by Christians in theology and in pastoral practice? The prevalent teaching of the Catholic Church in this period was the classical doctrinal theology originating in the time of St Augustine and continued throughout the Middle Ages till at least the Second Vatican Council of 1962–65. The background presupposition was that all humanity is in a state of *original sin* – the sin of the first parents handed down from generation to generation by propagation. The only possibility of eternal salvation for humans was through the merits of the death of Jesus Christ on the cross communicated to humans by the Church through the sacrament of Baptism. This was the *Fall-Redemption theology* that explained human salvation in a exclusivist sense: salvation is only through the Church: '*extra ecclesiam nulla salus*'. Other religions that did not accept this position were considered erroneous and a danger to human salvation.

A corollary of this teaching was that since faith in the teachings of the Church was necessary for salvation, those who spread false teachings, or heresy, were a danger to the eternal salvation of others also. Just as the community authority had the right and duty to restrain those who are a danger to the lives of others, so also the church community could, if necessary, use force or appeal to state power to prevent the spread of heresy and the consequent eternal damnation of souls. On this basis the use of force for the spread of the true faith and the elimination of false religions was justified. There was thus an alliance between the colonial invaders and the missioners of Christ, who strengthened one another in their military, political, and economic enterprises and evangelizing mission.

Thus the churches collaborated in the spread of the western colonial empires in the rest of the world, and colonial rulers supported the missionary enterprise in the new areas opened by possibilities of travel and new weapons of armed conquest of territories, especially those of unarmed native peoples 'discovered' by Columbus and his successors. This alliance continued at least till the independence of the colonized peoples, and in some places even beyond that.

A Christian reflection would have to be fostered in which the Churches together – Protestant, Orthodox, Catholic – can reflect on this anomaly in which, instead of truly sharing property and wealth, the Christian peoples helped to increase and consolidate the inequalities in the world. This is a major challenge for several reasons. The still-prevailing traditional classical theology was wrong in claiming an exclusive monopoly of the path to salvation, and hence in its assessment of other religions. Now the growing right-wing Christian fundamentalism tends to accentuate this claim of exclusivity of salvation by Jesus Christ. The global media and the educational processes, including most faculties of theology, do not present these issues in their complete historical perspective. This tends to give a sense of satisfaction and complacency to the more affluent Christian peoples, who continue to benefit from past violence. *The real original sin of the modern West* lies in the fact that the centuries of brutal colonial expansion since 1492 constituted a world order that is gravely sinful.

The main inspiration of the present world order set up mainly by European expansion is not Jesus Christ and his teachings but rather the quest for wealth and power. The gold brought from the new world of the Americas and the slaves, mainly from Africa, gave the European peoples a head start in modern capitalist economic growth. The sinful world structure has been consolidated by the power of armaments and legitimated by certain concepts and norms of international law historically put in place after the wars of conquest and world wars of previous centuries. Is it not Mammon, alongside Mars the god of war, who has been the main inspiration of the modern West, rather than Jesus Christ?

This history, with its western Christian roots, captured the whole world and today represents a threat, mainly to the lives of poor people. And 'in this criminal history of Christianity, the responsibility falls, precisely, on the set of theoretical elements that made possible such arrogance' (R. Bernhard), in terms of an exclusivist theology that justified, often in the name of the salvation of others, invasion, conquest, domination, and control of the thought, freedom, and life of others. While western Christianity has lost the veneer/varnish of no longer being able to hide its true religious structure and perhaps the true root of the divinity that the West adores – the god of money and of war – the religious experience rooted among poor persons is part of their resistance and dignity.

Facing this, authentic Christianity, which certainly inhabited and persisted in the West, is called to a 'deconstruction' of that ancient exclusivist, and even inclusive, theology and to the construction of a new theology – humble, divested of superiority, that recognizes a pluralistic paradigm, that does not consider itself to be unique, or the centre, or the elected, or, even more, the only and absolute saviour of others, but the saviour 'with others, that considers itself to be a religious tradition among others, on the journey with others along the many paths of God'. Authentic Christianity is also called to a 'reversion', putting in its heart the lives of the many poor, with their different religious experiences in diverse religions.

But it is not only Christianity that is involved. All religious traditions, above all those that have greatly expanded, are today confronted with this common challenge: the lives of the poor and the life of the earth. It is life that celebrates God; this is the most sacred principle in all religious traditions. Christianity alone, so linked to the devastating history of the West, does not have the authority, competence, or capacity to take on this task. The great apartheid created by the original sin of the West, which 'punishes others', cannot be overcome by the West. It has to open itself to the religious energies of other traditions and learn from them. There is something in common that reflects the Golden Rule, which can reunite and rescue humanity: Compassion will save us. And Compassion does not know the limits of religion, nor the limits between religions: *Extra misericordiam, nulla salus.*

# Religious Pluralism as a New Paradigm for Religions

FAUSTINO TEIXEIRA

It is not just today that Christianity finds itself facing the basic challenge of religious pluralism. In an inaugural address dating from April 1961, a lecture given in Eichstätt in Bavaria, Karl Rahner spoke of the need for an 'open Catholicism' that would be capable of confronting the imperative of religious pluralism. At the time he said that this pluralism could not just be viewed as 'a factual given' but that it had to be taken seriously and situated in the 'vast and complex whole of the Christian conception of existence'.[1] Many years in advance of what is becoming an increasingly relevant subject for reflection, Rahner marked his distance from a 'theology of perfection' that reduced other religions to 'natural beliefs' and indicated the need to see 'substantial supernatural traces of grace' at the heart of every one of them. This opened the way to understanding the 'legitimacy' of the other religious traditions in the saving plan of God.[2] This new perspective was to be found not only in the field of Roman Catholic theology, but occurred also in the Protestant camp, among theologians such as Wolfhart Pannenberg and Paul Tillich. Shortly before his death, in a lecture given in October 1965 at Chicago University, Tillich opposed Karl Barth's theological outlook and courageously defended the revelatory and salvific presence of God in other religious traditions, affirming that these 'revelatory experiences' have universal human validity.[3]

But this advance in theological thinking was not followed by a similar openness in the realm of the Roman Catholic ecclesial magisterium. It is like the description in the fourth Gospel of Simon Peter after Jesus' resurrection: he runs together with John, but the latter moves faster to marvel at the mystery posed by the empty tomb (John 20.3–6). It is true that Vatican II had already taken a first opening step in accepting the worth of other religions, but Christian consciousness was still strongly marked with the power and seduction of the old axiom, '*extra ecclesia nulla salus*'. However much this adage had become an 'obscure formula' at the council,[4] it did not lose its staying power, as can seen from the use of its 'positive' re-formulation in the *Catechism of the Catholic Church*, where the formula is taken to mean that 'all salvation comes from Christ the Head through the Church which is his Body'.[5] The documents of the Roman Catholic ecclesial magisterium and of the theology that underpins it are still very marked by the presence of offensive and deleterious language with regard to other religious traditions. The maximum conceded to other religions is a 'longing' to know God.[6] The documents cling to the notion that they are 'natural religious expressions', which share in a dynamic of 'search' for God, but one that is qualitatively different from what takes place in Christianity, which is the only setting in which 'an authentic and living relationship with God' is to be found.[7] In an extreme form of this, the Declaration *Dominus Iesus* firmly states that followers of other religious traditions '*objectively* speaking . . . are in a gravely deficient situation in comparison with those who, in the Church, have the fullness of the means of salvation.'[8] The conviction expressed in several documents follows the line that '*the Church is the ordinary means of salvation* and that *she alone* possesses the fullness of the means of salvation' (RM 55; italics original); that it is the 'only true religion' (DI 23), toward which the different religious traditions are 'ordered' (LG 16).[9]

There are, therefore, highly visible difficulties and hurdles obstructing proclamation of an innovative theological reflection on religious pluralism in the ambit of Christian tradition, in the Roman Catholic tradition especially. And the arguments that reinforce the traditional view of the 'need' for the Church for salvation are joined by fear of religious pluralism, seen as a phenomenon that destabilizes 'what is self-evident to the senses' and ushers in the spread of a relativism that threatens identities. As Claude Geffré has shown, 'The Roman magisterium . . . has a horror of pluralism, which it views as an ideology that despairs of all truth and leads to relativism'.[10]

The present time, however, calls for a different outlook and sensitivity. There is no room in the age of religious pluralism for absolutizing narratives or dismissive language: 'At no other time have people had such a sense of the difference of others, of the pluralism of societies, of cultures and religions, as of the relativity this implies. It is no longer possible to postulate the centrality of western culture, the supremacy of its outlook, or Christianity as the superior religion, or Christ as the absolute centre in relation to which all other mediations are relative.'[11]

Taking proper account of pluralism, not just as a fact of the situation but as something of permanent worth, means discovering otherness, the irrevocable enigma of the other, which has so often been excluded from the major narratives. Christian theology today finds itself faced with the basic challenge of making a 'qualitative leap'. A real theological *metanoia* has become necessary, bringing about a triple purification mechanism: of memory, of language, and of theological understanding.[12] We have to move beyond the language of 'detachment' in favour of the quest for a new relationship in dialogue; we have to construct a new language of acceptance of otherness, characterized by delicacy and courtesy, respectful of the religious patrimony of others; we also have to find a new theological understanding, which can bring in a new way of grasping and considering the universe of the others. The greatest risk we run at the present time is not that of joint celebration but that of self-congratulatory centrality and demonizing of others. The basic challenge is to weave new ways capable of encouraging a broadening of our thinking and listening to enable us to discern with clarity.

## I. Religious pluralism as a new paradigm

Religious pluralism is an undeniable phenomenon of this twenty-first century and represents one of the most important challenges facing Christian theology. This is summoned to a radical hermeneutical about-face, in the sense of a creative re-appropriation or actualization of the Christian message in the face of the insuperable plurality of the mysterious ways that lead to ultimate reality. This is a difficult, demanding, and provocative task: the greater our knowledge of the teachings and practices of other religious traditions, the more tools we acquire for 'creative reinterpretation' of the truths that point up the singularity of the Christian faith.[13] It is quite appropriate to define this religious pluralism as a 'new theological paradigm',[14] in the sense that it implies a profound transformation of concepts and values.[15] Acceptance of religious pluralism as an irrevocable value involves an essential change to the 'overall constellation' of patterns and schemes that define the shape of self-understanding in a particular community and the dynamic of how it perceives its relationship with the ultimate mystery. It means moving beyond the actual situation in the direction of the possible, broadening what is 'available to believe' (*le croyable disponible*). The way in which the Christian faith is proclaimed at the present time does not always find plausible confirmation in people's actual experience. There is evidence of a mismatch between the content proclaimed, often described as 'the deposit', and the new evidence supplied by reason, which conforms to the 'available to believe'. This also applies to the way we evaluate other religious traditions. Hence the fundamental importance of distinguishing between what in fact defines the true object of faith and what betrays representations of the world linked to a particular period.[16]

Openness to and relationship with 'the other' activates the interpretative dynamic, facilitating perception of unseen elements that escape the field of vision of the common parlance of Christianity: 'There are, then, surprisingly "true", "good,", "beautiful" aspects to the various (human) forms of harmony with God, aspects that have no place in the specific experience of Christianity".[17] In the complex pattern of the changes of paradigm brought about within Christianity, Hans Küng identifies the present time as that of emergence of the contemporary ecumenical paradigm, which will come to replace the modern enlightenment paradigm.[18]

In dealing with a new paradigm, it becomes problematic to maintain the traditional repertory that insists on proclaiming Christianity as the one true religion, or on the Church as bearer of the fullness of the means of salvation, or even on Jesus Christ as the constitutive factor of universal salvation. This is not to deny the singular truth of Christianity, but it does mean denying its claim to absolutism. As seen from the inner perspective of the Christian faith, Jesus Christ still holds his normative place for 'Christian understanding of ultimate reality',[19] but this does not in any way exclude a positive evaluation of religious pluralism, to the extent that this keeps open access to the sense of the mystery of God's transcendence and of the several paths that are traced out in God's gracious puzzle. As Roger Haight points out, 'acceptance of God's universal saving influence transforms religious pluralism into a positive situation, in which we can learn more about ultimate reality and human existence than we can find available in one single tradition'.[20]

Accepting pluralism as a new paradigm for the religions means recovering the value of plurality and the wealth of diversity; it means accepting diversity as an expression of the 'wealth of human experience' and pluralism as one of the most enabling experiences known to human consciousness.[21] Despite the impediments posed by some documents of the *magisterium*, such as *Dominus Iesus* (see DI 4), there is growing conviction in theological circles that pluralism of principle should be upheld—a pluralism, that is, not tied to a contingent historical situation but forming part of God's mysterious design for humanity.[22] And this mystery, which escapes human grasp, is rooted in God's self-communicating and loving dynamic.

The vision opened up by religious pluralism of principle enables us to glimpse the universal and welcoming presence of ultimate mystery in all humankind and all creation. In truth, as Haight has pertinently observed, 'persons who are unable to accept the saving truth of other religions may implicitly be working with a concept of God separated from creation'.[23] Acceptance and welcome of the various religious paths and witnesses of other traditions comes with development of perception of God as creator. And this means also breaking with the negative image of the religions as lacking in revelatory presence, as though they were wrapped round by the 'void' of the Spirit. In fact, even before human beings came to a readiness to seek the greatest mystery, they were already embraced and surrounded by the gift of God's mercy. In reality, it was God 'who sought them first and traced out for them the paths they should follow in order to find him'.[24] One the great figures of Sufi mysticism, Jalálu'ddin Rúmí (C. 13), wrote in his *Masnaví* that not only do those who are thirsty look for water but water also seeks out all those in the world who are thirsty (v. 1740). It is sufficient just to appear thirsty for water to spring up all around you.

## II. Coming closer in depth

The new paradigm of religious pluralism places the summons to inter-religious hospitality at the centre of the debate. Openness to the other uncovers unique potentialities for approaching the plural mystery of God and the riches of God's infinite wisdom. Hospitality is the entrance gate and singular opportunity for 're-discovering God'.[25] And this re-discovery proceeds not on the surface but in the depths, as Paul Ricoeur, developing Paul Tillich, convincingly shows. His image of a sphere is an expressive illustration of this dynamic. While distances are greater if we take the circumference of the circle as a basis, they are shortened if we take a direct route through its centre. In other words, it is in deepening the undertaking, in rooting our commitment, that we create the necessary conditions for meeting others.[26] This route of coming closer in depth shows the importance of the mystic outlook for being able to access the mystery that underlies the dynamic of religious pluralism. Paul Tillich showed real understanding of this throughout the course of his theological reflection, which demonstrated the power of the Spiritual Presence[27] as the clearing horizon of religious ambiguity: 'Where the divine Spirit is more than religion, it prevents any claim to absolutism, both on the part of the Church and on that of its members. Where the divine Spirit is effective, the claim of a Church to represent God to the exclusion of the others is rejected. The freedom of the Spirit contradicts any such claim.'[28]

Those within Christianity who are working in the area of the mystical approach are reinforcing an ever clearer conviction that the deeper and farther they advance in religious experience made possible by tradition itself, the greater their consciousness that the Reality they experience cannot be limited to religion in itself. At the apogee of his theological reflection, Paul Tillich had a remarkable insight into this question when he pointed to the way of depth as the essential condition for moving beyond a limited feature of Christianity: this is not a way that leads to abandoning religious tradition itself but a deepening of it through prayer, thought, and action. For him, 'in the depths of every living religion there is a point where the religion itself loses its importance and the horizon toward which it is moving produces a breaking of its particularity, raising it to a spiritual freedom that makes possible a new view of the presence of the divine in all expressions of the ultimate meaning of human life.'[29]

There is no way of ignoring the effect produced by taking stock of religious pluralism of principle. It is something that calls for a 'new and global hermeneutic of the Christian faith', an open hermeneutic, ruled by the 'art of empathy'. All treatises of Fundamental Theology are turned upside down and summoned to the exercise of broadening their vision. Understanding of religious truth will also be enriched, perceived from then on as a dynamic in process: a 'plural truth' that will be unveiled in the course of inter-religious conversation. Religious pluralism does not just protect the irreducibility of the other; it also protects the sense of God's mystery and transcendence.

*Translated by Paul Burns*

*Notes*

1. Karl Rahner, 'Christianity and the Non-Christian Religions', in *Theological Investigations* 5, London: Darton, Longman & Todd, 1966 (here Ital. ed., 1965, p. 534).
2. *Ibid.*, p. 545.
3. Paul Tillich, *The Future of Religions*, New York: Harper & Row, 1966 (here Ital. ed., 1970, p. 118). In one of his four Bampton Lectures, delivered in 1961, still under the influence of his visit to Japan, Tillich pointed out that one of the essential conditions for any inter-religious dialogue was recognition of the strength of the others' religious conviction, and that this conviction was rooted in an 'experience of revelation': cf. Tillich, 'A Christian-Buddhist Conversation', ch. 3 of *Christianity and the Encounter of the World Religions*, Columbia University Press, 1963 (here Port. ed., p. 607).

4. Bernard Sesboüé, *Hors de l'Église pas de salut*, Paris: Desclée de Brouwer, 2004, p. 355. Sesboüé accepts that this formula is still found in Denziger as an 'official formula of the Catholic Church' and is still firmly held by many: *ibid.*, p. 365.

5. *Catechism of the Catholic Church*, Vatican online ed., ²1997, n. 846. Following the line of the theology of perfection, in speaking of other religions the *Catechism* can only recognize in them a 'search' for the unknown God and see what is good and true in them as a 'preparation for the Gospel': cf. n. 843.

6. John Paul II, *Redemptoris missio* (RM), n. 45.

7. Paul VI, *Evangelii nuntiandi* (EN), n. 5.

8. Congregation for the Doctrine of the Faith, *Dominus Iesus* (DI), n. 22.

9. The expression 'ordering to the people of God' is taken from *Mystici corporis* DzH 3821), based on Thomas of Aquinas (ST IIIa, q.8, a.3, ad 1): cf. Sesboüé, *op. cit.*, pp. 232, 315. In the Protestant sphere, Paul Tillich was to recognize a 'latency of Spiritual Community' in the other religious communities, which would guide them 'unconsciously to Christ' when encountering the missionary activity of the Christian Churches: cf. Tillich, *Systematic Theology*, vol. III, Chicago: Univ. of Chicago Press, 1963 (here Port. ed., p. 607).

10. Claude Geffré, 'The Crisis of Christian Identity in an Age of Religious Pluralism', *Concilium* 2005/3, p. 19.

11. Roger Haight, *Jesus, Symbol of God*, Maryknoll, NY: Orbis, 1999 (here Port. ed., pp. 385–6).

12. Jacques Dupuis, *Christianity and the Religions*, Maryknoll, NY: Orbis, 2001 (here Ital. ed., p. 474).

13. Geffré, 'Verso una nuova teologia delle religioni', in R. Gibellini (ed.), *Prospettive teologiche per il XXI secolo*, Brescia: Queriniana, 2003, p. 267; Dupuis, 'La teologia del pluralismo religioso revistata,' *Rassegna di Teologia*, XI, 5 (Sept.–Oct. 1999), p. 692.

14. Geffré, *Croire et interpréter*, Paris: Cerf, p. 9.

15. Hans Küng, *Declaration for a World Ethic*, 1992 (here Port. ed., 1992, pp. 39, 192); Monique Aebischer-Crettol, *Vers un oecuménisme interreligieux*, Paris: Cerf, p. 649.

16. Geffré, *Profession Théologien*, Paris: Albin Michel, 1999, p. 108.

17. Edward Schillebeeckx, *The Human Story of God*, New York: Crossroad, 1999 (here ital. ed., 1992, p. 220).

18. Küng, *Christianity: Essence, History, and Future*, New York: Continuum, 1995.

19. Haight, *Jesus, Symbol, op. cit..* p. 468.

20. *Ibid.*, p. 485. In Haight's view, 'the Christian experience of what God does in Jesus Christ cannot be said to be diminished by recognizing the true God working in other religions'. In fact, as he sees it, 'the fear that something will be lost if we conceive of God at work in other religions is based on a premiss of competition among religions': *ibid.*, pp. 474, 486.

21. Raimon Panikkar, *Entre Dieu et le cosmos. Entretiens avec Gwendoline Jarczyk*, Paris: Albin Michel, 1998, p. 166.

22. Schillebeckx, *Human Story, op. cit.*, pp. 92, 220; Dupuis, *Toward a Theology of Religious Pluralism*, Maryknoll, NY: Orbis, 1997 (here Ital. ed., 1997, pp. 518–20); Geffré, *Croire, op. cit.*, pp. 94–5; *idem.*, *De babel à pentecôte*. Paris: Cerf, 2006, p. 94. And from a viewpoint firmly based in Latin American theology, Faustino Teixeira, 'La teología del pluralismo religioso en América Latina', in J. M. Vigil, L. E. Tomota, and M. Barros (eds.), *Por los muchos caminos de Dios, IV*, Quito: Abya-Yala, 2006, pp. 20–21; José María Vigil, *Teología del pluralismo religioso*, Quito: Abya-Yala, 2005.

23. Haight, *Jesus, Symbol*, p. 379; Gavin D'Costa, 'Christ, Trinity and Religious Pluralism', in D'Costa (ed.), *Christian Uniqueness Reconsidered: The Myth of a Pluralistic Theology of Religions*, Maryknoll, NY: Orbis, 1990 (here Ital. ed., 1994, p. 97).

24. Dupuis, *Christianity, op. cit.*, p. 468.

25. D'Costa (ed.), *Christian Uniqueness, op. cit.* p. 10, n. 36.

26. Paul Ricoeur, *Lectures I*, Paris: Seuil, 1991 (here Port. ed., 1995, pp. 188–9); Christian Duquoc, *L'unique Christ*, Paris: Cerf, 2002, p. 125.

27. '[This Spiritual Presence] through which the individual is possessed in the act of faith transcends conditions, beliefs, and expressions of individual faith': Tillich, *Systematic Theology III, op. cit.*, p. 607.

28. Tillich, *ibid.*, p. 687.

29. Tillich, *Christianity and the Encounter, op. cit.*, p. 173; Jean-Marc Aveline, *L'enjeu christologique en théologie des religions*, Paris: Cerf, 2003, p. 658 and v. 551–2; Paul F. Knitter, *Introduction to Theologies of Religions*, Maryknoll, NY: Orbis, 2002 (here Ital. ed., 2005, pp. 252–3).

# II. Discernment

# The Pluralist Paradigm: Tasks for Theology Toward a Pluralist Re-reading of Christianity

This issue of *Concilium* deals with religious pluralism as the challenging 'emerging paradigm'. My assignment is to tackle specifically the tasks and the challenges this new paradigm implies for Christian theology and for the theoretical representation of religions in general.

## I. 'Pluralist theology' rather than 'theology of religious pluralism'

We speak of 'paradigm', a familiar concept derived from the scientific world, warmly welcomed in theology and religious studies in general. A paradigm is the global model, the preconception around which the overall concept organizes itself. So the hypothesis I start from is this: in our history we have moved into a 'change of paradigm', which is coming about in culture as a whole and also affects the religions, Christianity among them, and within this, logically, theology too.

We are, however, dealing here with a regional matter within theology. 'Theology of religious pluralism' is effectively, in its first meaning, simply a new name for 'theology of religions', the origin of which many would trace to H. R. Schlette's *Towards a Theology of Religions*.[1]

This theology has produced different classifications of the various models that can be adopted in thinking through the relationship among religions. The simplest and most pedagogical is the tripartite approach of J. P. Schineller: exclusiveness, inclusiveness, and pluralism – three different

ways of conceiving the relationship among religions, and therefore three
different ways of doing theology: exclusivist theology, inclusivist theology
. . . or pluralist theology.

What, then, would a 'pluralist theology' be like? It would no longer be a
'genitive' or sectional theology, like the theology 'of' (or on) pluralism. Its
object of concern would no longer be the 'plurality' of religions. Pluralist
theology deals with 'everything', since it is not 'a branch'; it is a type, a genre
of theology specified by the pluralist paradigm. Pluralist theology is the new
form into which the whole of the old theological edifice can be re-cast. It is
the new paradigm from which to 're-write all theology', as Paul Tillich
expressed as his wish a few days before his sudden death during a conference
that was to become his theological testament.[2] So it is no longer just a matter
of doing a theology of pluralism (= plurality) of religions, but of re-writing
all theology from the new viewpoint (or formal object) of pluralism (= paradigm opposed to exclusiveness and inclusiveness).

The pluralist paradigm affects not only theologies, the theoretical representations of religions, but the religions themselves. It is the actual lived
experience of religion and spirituality that can be exclusivist, inclusivist, or
pluralist. The future I envisage is, therefore, a 'pluralist Christianity',
toward which we are heading, leaving behind the present inclusivist
Christianity, which in its turn displaced the previous form of Christianity,
the exclusivist one. The transformation unleashed by the new paradigm is
all-embracing; it affects not only theology but also spirituality, evangelization, pastoral work, social teaching, and even politics: we are moving toward
an overall reality, 'pluralist Christianity'.

## II. Tasks for theology

So, way beyond a merely sectional 'theology of religious pluralism', what is
under way today is the upsurge of the theology of pluralism in the sense of
'pluralist theology', which is not limited to a theme or branch of theology but
seeks to re-read the whole structure of theology, as a whole and in each of
its branches. What are the major tasks involved in constructing this global
theological edifice? I should select the following:

### (a) Sincere acceptance of pluralism as a paradigm

Both exclusiveness and inclusiveness were, by their nature, opposed to
religious pluralism. This was held to be – implicitly, above all – a negative,

sinful situation, contrary to the will of God. Mythically, it derived from the punishment inflicted by God himself for the sin of human pride, when he confused languages, so giving rise to cultural and religious diversity (Babel). . . . So religious pluralism was the fruit of sin and could not conceivably be viewed as part of God's plan.

The construction of pluralist theology implies the theological task of recognizing and welcoming the sensitivity through which people today perceive pluralism as something positive, as a reflection of the infinite riches of God. Specifically religious pluralism corresponds to the will of God and should be accepted with gratitude, instead of being rejected or opposed.

This task is not theological only but affects all aspects of life: it is a matter of effectively incorporating the positive evaluation of religious pluralism into the entire life of the community. Among Catholics, for example, the Roman Missal, the heart of official liturgical spirituality, is entirely ignorant of religious pluralism: other religions are not even mentioned in prayer,[3] except in the 'Mass for the Evangelization of Peoples', which presents them as a plurality of religions that must be reduced to the unity of 'a single flock under a single shepherd'.

### (b) A pluralist re-reading of the theology of revelation

The theology of 'revelation' itself, in its totality, is probably most in need of a theological re-working that will move beyond the residues of fundamentalism that still lead so many believers to take exclusivist and inclusivist biblical statements as coming materially from God, and therefore being literally untouchable and un-interpretable. There is a need to deepen and to consolidate the re-interpretation that is already in progress on many academic theological levels, but which has not yet penetrated the Christian faithful or the institutional structures of the Churches, which cling (in their own interest) to fundamentalist interpretations.

A 'pluralist' interpretation of revelation would frame it in the multiple and irreducible work of God in all religions, which produces and advances human processes of maturation and appropriation of the religious life-experience of peoples. The written codification of those experiences – the scriptures – bring us close to the religious sensibility with which those earlier generations responded to the transcendent Mystery, to which we too today should give our own response, as free and creative as that of those generations, taking advantage of their witness, but without becoming hostages to the 'beliefs' included in their testimony, by taking them as God's word and not also as human creation and/or spontaneous historic phenomena. A pluralist theology of revelation still remains to be worked out.

## (c) Renunciation of the 'chosen' category

The belief that we are the nation and/or religion chosen by God, unlike all the others, has been an illusion common to religions.

Renouncing the doctrine and understanding of 'exclusiveness' is something that no longer surprises or 'shocks' us today, because although it was a doctrine held to and believed in with maximum intolerance (the death sentences handed down by the Inquisition) and supreme generosity (martyrs for the faith) over nineteen centuries, it has already been abandoned and officially denied, and today we can say that it has been swallowed and forgotten. On the other hand, renouncing the doctrine and understanding of being 'chosen' still meets a great deal of resistance today. So Andrés Torres Queiruga's call to Catholics to 'renounce the concept of being chosen' is both prophetic and truly programmatic.[5]

This is an urgent task for theology, and even for society, since only religions that move beyond their self-conviction of being 'the chosen ones' can come together in an 'alliance of civilizations' (and of religions) to tackle together the practical tasks of saving the human race and saving the planet.

## (d) Re-reading Christology in a pluralist age

It is strange but true that while Jesus of Nazareth – his message, his behaviour, his actions . . . as presented in the Gospels – pose no problems to a pluralist Christianity (or *Jesuanity*), it is the image of Christ elaborated in the Christological dogmas of the fourth to fifth centuries that turn out to be the *punctum dolens* for devising a pluralist Christology.

A prime aspect of this task is revising the Christocentric exclusiveness that lies at the bottom of the normal interpretation of inclusiveness. As a matter of course, christological dogma was elaborated within an exclusivist outlook, which is no longer sustainable. For many centuries the umbrella dogma of Christology also sheltered exclusiveness, and this was generally held to be dogma too. Christianity was able to shake off this 'dogma' and make the leap to inclusiveness only when exclusiveness became no longer credible in the general cultural consciousness, in the late twentieth century. It will be able to make the leap toward a 'pluralist' Christology when a pluralist epistemology becomes more deep-seated in society's cultural consciousness and thence permeates religions – a process already under way and indeed already accomplished in many areas. In the meanwhile, the ongoing theological task is to prepare for opening new ways or paths for building a pluralist theology.[6]

There is no doubt that Christology is currently the most urgent of all the theological endéavours involved in developing a pluralist theology and a pluralist Christianity.

### (e) Rethinking mission from a pluralist theological standpoint

Today, when pluralist theology accepts that all religions are basically valid responses to the Divine Mystery, and that their plurality, rather than being a bad thing, corresponds to the divine plan, mission still has meaning, but a different meaning. It can no longer claim to be struggling against religious plurality and reducing it to unity, nor to be strictly one-directional (going only to teach without expecting to learn anything), nor to be proposing proselytism or conversion. Pluralist mission does not set out to convert members of other religions but seeks to see them living the religion in which God has placed them more fully. It does not only claim to teach but also seeks to learn. Reconstruction of a new, pluralist, missiology is another current task for theology.

### (f) Many poor, many religions

Religious pluralism is also a challenge to contextual and liberative theologies – as all should be. Latin American liberation theology, for example, is trying to incorporate the challenge that Aloysius Pieris addressed to it: this theology, which so elegantly conveys its good news to the continent's poor, becomes irrelevant on the world scene – so he said – because demographically speaking most of the world's poor are not Christian but live among an enormous plurality of religions: many are the poor and many are their religions. Latin American liberation theology is, he said, 'a luxury for a Christian minority'; if theology is going to speak to the poor, it needs to do so in the language of the many religions of the poor. . . .

So we need an inter-religious theology that speaks to the poor of the world in their language, which is inter-religious. This challenge, which comes from Asia, has led Latin America's Ecumenical Association of Third World Theologians (EATWOT) to devote the last five years to devising an encounter between its liberation theology and the theology of religious pluralism, which was previously unknown in the Latin American sphere.[7]

Once this effort has met with results, I believe we shall need to take further steps forward:

– set the sights of theology on the salvation of the poor and the salvation of  the earth;
– ask the religions each to face up to this double salvation and express it in its own theological language;
– share what emerges in common: an 'inter-religious theology' of liberation;
– add together all the elements particular to each religion that bring contributions to the common search for this double salvation: a 'multi-religious theology' of liberation;
– dare to venture down a new path that alarms many: a 'trans-religious theology' of liberation: that is, a theology that on the one hand can be grasped and applied in each religion and on the other can try to build, in a spirit of communion with all religions, an environment, a setting, a language, categories, a 'theology' . . . that can be a common patrimony of humanity, situated beyond actual religions, in a 'simply human spirituality', lay, 'post-religion', trans-religious. . . .
– succeed in putting all the religions to work, together, at what must be the most urgent need today: saving the lives of the poor and saving the life of the planet, and doing so on the ethical basis of the 'golden rule'. This would be today's best expression of the theology of religious pluralism and of inter-religious dialogue.

Alongside all this, for some times voices within EATWOT have been pointing out the need for a new association, no longer 'ecumenical' but trans-religious, and no longer of the Third World but of the whole world – though, of course, starting from the option for the poor. The project is in hand.

## III. What do these challenging tasks imply?

### (a) A theological revolution

First and foremost they imply a theological revolution the like of which has not been seen in twenty centuries of Christianity. This is because exclusiveness and inclusiveness still have a lot in common; inclusiveness is still a formally tempered exclusiveness, tolerant toward other religions, not entirely denying them the presence of salvation, but nevertheless still upholding the exclusively privileged and prime position held by Christianity on the chart of salvific efficacy.

The leap from inclusiveness to pluralism, on the other hand, supposes the abandonment of this common ground of privilege and superiority from which we have not yet budged. Accepting a re-reading of Christianity in a pluralist key means accepting 'believing in a different way': in a despoiled, de-throned, humbled, kenotic way. It means being Christian while renouncing the 'myth of religious superiority',[8] the understanding that we are 'the' true religion, the absolute, the one whose saving powers all others share in, even without being conscious of doing so, the one for which all others are merely a *preparatio Evangelii*, the one into which all others will have to flow at the end of time, the one that represents the supreme human form of religious expression and is the greatest embodiment of religious reasoning, the one religion outside which human beings are in 'a gravely deficient situation for salvation'. . . .

This is effectively a theological revolution. Not a lateral, partial, or sectional shift, but a total one, across the board. A revolution. A new Christianity? A post-Christianity? Can the inclusive Christianity keep its same identity in the pluralist one? This is another subject still to be debated in a future issue of *Concilium*.

### (b) This is not all there is at stake.

Even though what is happening in the advance of the new pluralist paradigm is very important, it is not all there is at stake in the current transformation of Christianity; there are many other complex questions coming to light and demanding so many other forthcoming changes. Here are a few such problems, by way of example:[9] the fact of having changed from being the 'Jesus movement' to an institutional religion and the state religion of the Roman Empire; having metamorphosed its essence to the extent of changing it almost exclusively into a doctrine and an institution; having entirely forgotten the mystagogic dimension and transmitting not religious experience but doctrinal catechesis; being still obsessively concerned with quantity and social power instead of quality even in a minority; not succeeding in accepting loss of the social power it enjoyed as inheritor of the empire and as single and official religion of Christendom. . . .

### (c) Nor is it the last change of paradigm.

The pluralist change is clearly not the last change of paradigm we are facing, but just another one making its entrance. I refer to the post-religion paradigm. The frightening religious crisis in Europe needs its own theological reflection, now that anthropological–cultural sciences are showing us a different focus from the official 'catastrophist' one. What is taking place is a social revolution comparable to the agrarian one at the dawn of the Neolithic period, which proved one of the most traumatic and fruitful moments in the history of humankind. That was when humankind formed its new religious consciousness, and that was the starting point for all the great religions as we still know them today.

The new interpretation put forward in anthropological and cultural studies[10] conjectures that the root of the present situation lies in the crisis of what has been the model of agrarian societies. The 'religions' were the form in which the perennial spirituality of the human race crystallized when agricultural society took shape. Europe is today the first society on the planet in which the last traces of the agrarian society are disappearing, and that is why the religions are in crisis there.

This new interpretation would then require us to re-conceptualize religion itself, since it will no longer appear to be identified with and equivalent to the spirituality of human beings but only with one of its forms, that which corresponded to a form of human life together, agrarian society, which is now disappearing. If it is possible that religions will disappear, we need to begin to work out the change human spirituality needs to make if it is to become 'post-religious'. This is another 'emerging paradigm', already happening in considerable portions of the planet, and one that EATWOT's International Theological Commission invites *Concilium* to tackle in an issue in the near future.

*Translated by Paul Burns*

## Notes

1. H. R. Schlette, *Towards a Theology of Religions* (Quaestiones disputatae), London and New York: Burns & Oates; Herder & Herder, 1966.
2. 'The Significance of the History of Religions for the Systematic Theologian', in J. C. Brauer (ed.), *The History of Religious Ideas*, New York: Herder & Herder, 1966.
3. This is what I have called 'the only son syndrome': see J. M. Vigil, *Teología del pluralismo religioso. Curso sistemático de teología popular*, Córdoba and Quito: El Almendro; Abya Yala, 2005, p. 100.
4. Andrés Torres Queiruga proved a qualified exponent of this in his *La revelación de Dios en la realización del hombre*, Madrid: Cristiandad, 1987.
5. *Idem*, 'El diálogo de las religiones en el mundo actual', in J. Gomís (ed.),

*Vaticano III. Cómo lo imaginan 17 cristianos y cristianas*, Bilbao: Desclée de Brouwer, 2001, pp. 70ff.

6. In the Declaration *Dominus Iesus* (3, 14), the then Cardinal Ratzinger invited theologians to consider 'some fundamental questions that remain open to further development'.

7. See the series 'Por los muchos caminos de Dios', part of the 'Tiempo axial' collection, Quito: Abya Yala, at latinoamericana.org/tiempoaxial.

8. Cf. Paul F. Knitter, *The Myth of Religious Superiority*, Maryknoll, NY: Orbis, 2005.

9. Carlos Palacio, 'El cristianismo en América Latina. Discernir el presente para preparar el futuro', *RELaT* (*Revista Electrónica Latinomaericana de Teología*), at servicioskoinonia.org/relat/372.htm.

10. Marià Corbí, 'Análisis epistemológico de las configuraciones axiológicas humanas' (thesis, univ. of Salamanca, 1983), in *Religión sin religión*, Madrid: PPC, 1996, and in the *virtual* library of Koinonia Services at www.servicioskoinonia.org/biblioteca.

# From Revelation to Revelations

PAULO SUESS

## I. The journey from revelations to revelation

The theological-pastoral concern of this article is acceptance of the poor-other, whether they are Christians or not, into the religious field of multiple Christianities as well as into the civil sphere. The poor-other are not only recipients of universal salvation in Jesus Christ; they are also universal bearers of God's revelation. This acceptance is not something external to the essentials of Christianity and therefore a strategic or tactical method of defending the cause of the poor and, in Latin America, that of the indigenous peoples; it is rather inherent in the gospel precepts. In Christianity, the social question is closely linked to the question of orthodoxy, and sin means indifference to the exploitation and neglect of the poor-other.

The argumentation of this article begins with a historical process that moves from revelations to the revelation that for Christians is essentially set out in the writings of the New Testament, the better to establish this link between the crucified of history and the ethical imperatives of the gospel, which seek to contextualize redemption, peace, and justice as its core values. This revelation in the plural of the biblical texts was again codified in the treatises of Fundamental Theology, which were faced with a number of revelations ongoing through history, codified in other cultural and religious keys. In the Church, the various revelations and codifications find a *locus* of discernment and of consensual objectivization, which pronounces on the salvific value or otherwise of the other ways and, necessarily, opens out on to the eschatological horizon on which the many experiences of God will come together in a unique and definitive revelation of God, without institutional mediation by religions or Churches.

From the dawn of humankind we have accounts of a God who revealed himself in many different ways to human beings, through either reason or intuition, through natural or historical phenomena, through his word addressed to ordinary people and prophets, within and outside Israel (cf.

Heb. 1.1ff). In most religions the experience of God exists as experience of God's revelation. In a first phase, the voice of God is received and transmitted orally. In the Judeo-Christian tradition the primordial process of God's self-revelation was taken up again in Israel's journey, described in the Old Testament, then later in God's project in Jesus Christ, later fixed in writing, according to the understanding and context of the various writers and theologies of the New Testament. Finally, this self-revelation was systematized in the different theologies of revelation down to our own days, when we are faced not only with a plurality of historical revelations but also with widely differing codifications of these revelations.

To emphasize this plurality of revelations, we can appeal to an authoritative voice that states, for example, that neither the Fathers nor medieval theologians such as Bonaventure had a concept of the question of 'essence of revelation' in the sense in which it is used in treatises of Fundamental Theology today. Revelation is always a synthetic abstraction of many actual revelations that are specific forms of experiencing God. 'Bonaventure knows of and deals with many detailed revelations, which took place over the course of salvation history, but he never raises the question of the single revelation that came about through these multiple revelations.'[1] Revelation, in this context, is a concrete act, an event, in which God reveals himself to a subject. Revelation as an act of God directed to persons is prior to and greater than what is established in the scriptures.

My intention here is to take us back to the act and the subjects of revelations that are contextualized and developed through 'word' and 'history' into different realities and theologies of revelation. This is, to an extent, a matter of taking up and expanding the hermeneutic work already present in the New Testament writers. Paul and John adopt traditional understandings of revelation and produce a new theological interpretation to explain God's salvific actions in Jesus Christ aimed at and starting from the context of a particular audience. Today, such an interpretation, and ecclesial discernment itself, have to take account of the connections between God's revelation in Jesus Christ and the continuity of revelations in history and in non-Christian religions.

The universality of salvation codified in revelation and in historical contingency as its setting points to the eschatological horizon of the world and of revelation itself in ever-developing historical conditions. This perspective enables us to think about the finality and end of religions and of the Church itself. Jesus Christ is not only the one who came but also the one who is to come, not only as judge, but as definitive revealer of the Father and giver of the grace of the unity of all humankind in the Holy Spirit, in accordance with God's desire for universal salvation. The same perspective enables us to think also of the definitive fulfilment of the deep meaning of revelation, which the 'here and now' of history does not allow us to do: God will remove the veil from his mystery. All will see God face-to-face, and absolute transcendence will become palpable in absolute proximity.

## II. The poor-other, recipients and subjects of revelation

In a prayer of praise, Jesus Christ thanks his disciples who have returned from their mission. Rejoicing in the Holy Spirit, he thanks the Father for having revealed the mystery of the kingdom to the little people: 'I thank you, Father, Lord of heaven and earth, because you have hidden these things from the wise and the intelligent and have revealed them to infants' (Luke 10.21; cf. Matt. 11.25). What is meant by 'these things'? The little people, the poor, the crucified of history are bearers of divine wisdom and have already received the revelation necessary for building God's purpose, which is the kingdom. They received revelation not because of their religious adherence but because of their social standing as 'infants'. Through the action of the Holy Spirit, Jesus invokes God as Creator of the universe and as Father, and he rejoices. The poor have always experienced the mystery of the Trinity through openness to God's purpose. The two universal affirmations made in this passage are that God is creator of the universe and that since the beginnings of humanity his revelation has been made not to 'the wise and the intelligent' but to 'infants'. According to God's designs, the dividing line between the success or failure of the disciples' mission, and of Jesus', does not set the good apart from the bad, saints from sinners, orthodox Jews from heterodox Samaritans, but divides the wisely presented ideology of the elites from the rough speech of the ordinary people, religious irrelevance from relevance (cf. Luke 10.25ff). For Jesus of Nazareth, revelation lies in the intuitive understanding of the folly of God as true wisdom. All God's wisdom, however, and his revelation as God's kingdom in our midst, is, despite and because of its historical specificity, an eschatological horizon. Jesus himself, the one who reveals, whose presence in history is a central point but at the end of revelation, can be understood only within this vision of definitive revelation in the *parousia*, freed from historical and cultural contingencies. These specifics can be stated:

- From the beginnings, the revelation of the creator God is accepted in all peoples, their cultures and religions. 'God provides all people, in created things, with a permanent testimony of himself (cf. Rom. 1.19f)' (DV 2). The non-ideological transmission of revelation is guaranteed to the victims of history.
- The more specific revelation in Jesus Christ, experienced in the different Christianities, is historically and culturally transmitted and, therefore, received in conditions of precariousness and ambivalence. In the *parousia*, the Word made flesh will be the Word of all tongues. In this universal Word all religions will accept each other and Christianity too will recognize the desires of the religions of others in Him. In this perspective, the question of truth, which is important above all for the universal religions, is not set aside but placed on the apocalyptic horizon of the gospel itself, and Christianity is set free from the confusion between its historical singularity and an absolute and a-historical exclusivity.
- The revelation of the end times can and should be hoped for as definitive revelation of the mysteries, as much for Christians as for the followers of other religions. For Christians, the subject of the parousia bears one of the many names humanity has given to God: Jesus Christ, which means God the Saviour and Messiah. In the eschatological perspective that should be envisaged as the end times and the end of cultural differentiations, we can speak of a coming together of opposites or differences that have so far prevented the definitive unveiling of the mysteries of God.

## III. The link between truth and poverty

The addressees of the word of God and the choice of protagonists of God's plan reveal the purpose and show the mediation of this plan. In a world of social inequality, exclusion of the poor, and commercialization or neglect of others, a revelation whose addressees were an ethic group or randomly selected individuals would run the risk of turning into the ideology of a privileged hegemonic group. It is easy to demonstrate this by looking at the sanctuaries that have sprung up from 'private revelations', whether accepted by the Church or not. For the elites these have become places of public prestige and opportunities for enrichment.

Jesus of Nazareth chose the little ones/others as the protagonists of his project, which is a world for everyone. In his core discourses in the synagogue at Nazareth (Luke 4), on the Beatitudes (Matt. 5), and on the Last Judgment (Matt. 25) Jesus makes himself very clear. The first and privileged recipients of his word, the protagonists and central nucleus of his project, which is the kingdom of God, are the victims and those 'naturally' disadvantaged. But the victims are not just protagonists or addressees of God's project; they are also God's representatives in the world and, as such, bearers and mediators of God's revelation and promise. The poor-other as protagonists and mediators of the kingdom are a universal category, irrespective of their ethnic, national, or cultural particularities.

The Churches need to learn that Jesus of Nazareth did not impose burdens on the weak or exclusion on the poor or compulsory inclusion on others. Jesus of Nazareth, the Messiah anointed by the Holy Spirit, criticized the deprivation of the poor and outsiders by the Synagogue. This deprivation also means depriving God of God's own word. So too the Church possesses an adequately true doctrine in the proximity of the poor. There is a link between truth and poverty.

In a fine passage, the then Cardinal Ratzinger quotes Plato's defence of Socrates, in which he points to his credibility in defending a god whose defence brings him no social or material reward: 'And I have a witness to the truth of what I say; my poverty is a sufficient witness'.[2] In Christianity, this witness is the poverty of God himself in the incarnation, in the manger, on the cross, and in the eucharistic bread. 'Poverty is the true divine appearance of the truth', wrote Ratzinger.[3] I should make an addition from Latin American theology: poverty in its actuality of the poor. In them, who are the setting for the epiphany and revelation of God, the Church recognizes 'the image of its poor and suffering Founder' (LG 8c), and through them Christ himself cries out in a loud voice (cf. LG 22a). Vatican II did not only read solidarity as incarnation (cf GS 32); it also read solidarity as saving recognition of the religious mystery that surrounds the poor (LG 16).

The pilgrims of Latin America discern their crucified and raised founder in the crucified of history. In his 'History of the Indies', Las Casas reported from distant Valladolid: 'I left in the Indies Jesus Christ, our God, scourged, afflicted, beaten, and crucified, not once, but a thousand times, by the Spaniards who are devastating and destroying those peoples [. . .].[4] In the Puebla Conclusions the suffering and revealing features of Christ are enumerated in terms of the real world of today (cf. 31ff).

## IV. Back to revelations

Vatican II added the paradigm of the missionary essence of all pastoral action to that of the territorial nature of missions, of 'having' missions, emphasizing the nature or 'missionary being' of the Church. The previous emphasis on 'having' missions drew an institutional line of demarcation between truth and falsehood, between the saved and the damned, between orthodoxy and heterodoxy. Exemplary missionaries such as Francis Xavier (1506–52) in Asia and Joseph of Anchieta (1491–1556) in Brazil shared the official teaching rooted in the territoriality of the Christendom-Church. When they left Europe, these missionaries already knew, from the manuals of theology, that the world of the other, of non-Catholics, was a world without grace and that they were going to implant the Church in these territories. The hermeneutical principles of this missionary activity are well known: (a) Christianity in its Catholic embodiment is the only religion that saves; (b) the religions of others are idolatrous religions because they are not founded on the revelation of the true God, so there is no salvation in them; (c) obtaining the salvation of souls is an urgent task for the Church; (d) the purpose of inter-religious dialogue is to convince others of their errors and convert them to Christianity; (e) salvation is an absolute good and, even if it brings physical suffering, as in the regime of slavery, is preferable to freedom outside Christianity.

When the Japanese asked him about the destiny of their ancestors, Francis Xavier had to reply that they were all in hell and that there was no spiritual way to save them.[5] Vatican II corrected this teaching on two points. It stated: (a) that freedom is the presupposition of mission (DH 2) and (b) that those who through no fault of their own do not know the Good News of Christ can be saved in their own religion (cf. LG 16 and AG 7a). But Vatican II also stated that Jesus Christ is the only mediator of salvation (cf. LG 8a; 14a) and that 'the one true religion is found in the Catholic Church' (DH 1b). The council therefore provide us with two different paths. As had happened in the early councils, Vatican II also failed to harmonize the theological tension inherent in the question. In the post-conciliar period, one of the theological currents, which became the prevailing one, attempted to close this open road.

In the encyclical *Redemptoris Missio* (1990) the two paths of Vatican II no longer exist. One way was put forward as *the* way (cf. RM 9). The 'declaration' *Dominus Iesus* (DI; 2000) is still more restrictive and on this point makes clear its aim to supersede the dialectic of Vatican II: (a) Jesus Christ is the sole saviour; (b) the followers of other religions can be saved, but not through their religions, which are not of divine origin; (c) these religions do not possess the power to save *ex opera operato*, which is confined to the Catholic sacraments (cf. DI 21); (d) salvation in other religions can come about with a special grace from Jesus Christ, which followers of these religions reach through the mediation of the Catholic Church.

Within the theological community and in local Churches, especially in Asia, *Dominus Iesus* did not succeed in imposing a consensus. On the contrary, the colonial tone of such statements created a generalized unease in the Churches that live in inter-religious contexts. Beyond some hermeneutical devices, universal ecclesial reception of *Dominus Iesus* did not take place. Discussion, based on Vatican II, will continue, as experiences of God, once more becoming revelation in the religions, continue. The only way for Christians and non-Christians to talk about God is by analogy. This holds both for the actual concepts of revelation within both Christianity and the other religions, which vary from natural revelation to varying forms of positive revelation. The intrinsic relationship between revelation and faith, which Christians proclaim, points to the fact that revelation can be understood only by starting from a certain interiority and familiarity, based on an internal logic and hermeneutics belonging to each religious system.

The continuity of revelation, outside the nucleus synthesized in Fundamental Theology, consists not in new contents but in the ever-new contextual and historical experiences of the Creator Word, who is still relevant not only on the basis of the incarnation but before and after it, not only for Israelites and Christians but also for those outside Israel or outside the Catholic Church, such as the Samaritans, the centurions, the widow of Zarephath, and lepers, such as Naaman the Syrian. The fact that the revelation to Israel did not reach all peoples does not mean that they are excluded from God's saving action. By analogy, the same could be said of those peoples and cultures in which Christianity has not succeeded in taking root. On the basis of God's will to save, we have to think of the ways put forward by the religions as routes that allow provisional access to salvation. This is also true of the Church itself. In historical-cultural situations, the absolute and definitive is always experienced in temporary and provisional form. The eschatological reserve is matched by the salvific reserve of God, who addresses himself freely and along many paths to the whole of humankind, without diminishing the saving role of Israel or the Church. The apostolic succession is an element imposing order within the Catholic Church, not an instrument that deprives God of his saving freedom. Genealogy, on its own, can prove ecclesiality but not, necessarily, orthodoxy. From the earliest days of humankind to the present, God has ways of communicating salvation outside each Church or religion. For the Church too, the truth is a horizon, not a possession (cf. DV 8b).

## V. Opening paths

The evolution from understanding of revelation as object of faith to understanding of revelation as God's salvific action in history and self-communication, at Vatican II; the evolution from the saving exclusivity of the Church, in Francis Xavier's time, to a dialectical understanding of several routes to salvation: all this indicates the historical nature of the Church's magisterium itself. This historical nature allows us to imagine – five hundred years from now, who knows? – the possibility of coming together with other religions, bearing truth not in boxes with weighty and rigid fundamentalist contents but, once again, as at the start, with the lightness of those poor fishermen, in clay vessels. Let us dream of Churches that will be places where belonging to a society will equate with belonging to a religion.

In God's terms, we are all eternal learners. We need to learn to lay stress on the sovereignty of God, saviour of the human race, radically incarnated in historical reality and, at the same time, radically transcendental, before and beyond all cultural, religious, and geographical contingencies. We can take the step from the territoriality of mission to the missionary nature of the Church, the People of God. We can embrace the priority of the practice of love over denominational orthodoxy, as explained in the parable of the Good Samaritan. We can rejoice in the saving revelation that Jesus of Nazareth attributed to the poor-others in his discourse on the Last Judgment. When we are tempted to weed out all the darnel of history, the Church reminds us of the eschatological horizon of revelation. We are still learners, listening to and receiving the word, as we hear ever anew the voice of God in his one saving design and, at the same time, in the multiplicity of echoes from the religions. We have come a long way. But these echoes and waves have still not been collectively understood by the majority of Churches. Walls that fall down are rebuilt. We live in an age of stonemasons. Let us look for carpenters who know how to make and open doors, like the carpenter from Nazareth.

*Translated by Paul Burns*

### Notes

1. Joseph Ratzinger, *Die Geschichtstheologie des heiligen Bonaventura*, St Ottilien: EOS, 1992, p. 59.
2. Plato, *Apology*, 31c. (trans. Benjamin Jowett).

3. Joseph Ratzinger, 'Der Dialog der Religionen und das jüdisch-christliche Verhältnis', in *idem*, *Die Vielfalt der Religionen und der Eine Bund*, Bäd Tolt: Urfeld, ³2003, pp. 93–121, here 116.

4. Bartolomé de Las Casas, *Historia de las Indias*, 3 vols., Caracas: Biblioteca Ayachcho (108–10), 1986, vol. 3 (liv. III, cap. 138), p. 510.

5. Cf. F. Zubillaga, *Cartas y escritos de San Francisco Xavier*, Madrid: BAC, 1968, here doc. 96, p. 48.

# Dwellings of the Wind on Human Paths: Toward a Theology of Hiero-diversity

MARCELO BARROS

The first time that, in the early 1990s, I visited the Afro-Brazilian *Opô Afonjá* ('White House at the Old Sugar Mill') temple in Salvador, I did so in order to gain a better understanding of the 'other' the Black soul in Brazil was to me, but also to integrate dialogue with Afro culture into my spirituality of a Benedictine monk living among the poor. Now, the more I try to penetrate Afro-Brazilian culture of Yoruba origin, the more attracted I become to the religion this community practises and to which it invites me. This religion in no way calls my Christian faith into question, but it requires an effort to understand it thoroughly. Since I decided, as a Christian and a monk, to experience this insertion in the world of Candomblé, I have found that religious belief has led me back to a deep communion with the culture that serves as an expression of spirituality but is broader than religion. There is something ineffable about this experience, but I should nevertheless like to share some reflections that arise from it. In keeping with the Latin American method, I start with how this relationship between culture and religion shows itself in the world. I then seek to clarify some concepts and put forward a theological deepening of the notion of 'hiero-diversity', a term I first heard from Luiz Carlos Susin and José María Vigil and which strikes me as very apt for describing a new path that, in the world of today, human beings are called, one way and another, to follow.

## I. Ghosts and terrors of cultural and religious pluralism

There are ghosts that people imagine and sincerely believe they have seen flying through the air. Others are simply made up, though once people believe in them they seem to take on a life of their own. The shock and wave of fear some persons and institutions have created around cultural plurality and religious pluralism belong to this second group. We all know that the

49

world has always been pluralist. Nations have, from antiquity, had different cultures, which have sometimes managed to exist peaceably together and have at other times come into conflict – the latter, unfortunately, more frequent in history. This ancient phenomenon of cultural plurality, never-theless, became more widespread in the closing decades of the twentieth century and began to be seen in new way. The Italian writer Ennio Flavio says, 'We are living in a period of transition', and adds, ironically, 'as always'.[1] Our increasingly wicked international politics, which serves to aggravate poverty in the Third World and migrations, contributes to making cultural and religious pluralism take new forms and require more up-to-date interpretations.

In the 1990s Samuel Huntington formulated his thesis that in this new century wars would be clashes of civilizations.[2] The cultural and religious diversity present on all latitudes of the planet gives the lie to this theory. Amartya Sen comments, for example, that with the exception of Indonesia and Pakistan, India has the largest Muslim population in the world.[3] In 1965 Vatican II declared that it would be false to identify Christianity with western culture: 'There is a cultural plurality at the heart of Christianity' (AG 22). In Latin America, as in Africa and Asia, the resurgence of many indigenous and peasant movements that reach across several cultures shows the falsity of this pessimistic theory, which is ultimately ethnocentric and colonialist.

## II. Going beyond concepts

According to Tylor's definition, 'culture is a complex whole that includes knowledge, beliefs, art, morality, laws, customs, and other capacities a human being acquires as a member of a society'.[4] Cardinal Ratzinger has summed this up by saying; 'Culture is the form of community expression historically developed by the acquisitions and judgments that characterize the life of a community.'[5]

One of the most common and important expressions of a culture is that which refers to the relationship between human beings and the ultimate mystery. In many ancient cultures, this dimension is so central and embraces all aspects of life to such an extent that there is no real organized religion as a separate sector. The activities and functions of life are imbued with this relationship to mystery. Worship is an important occasion and has its own special persons and rites, but they are not exclusive. Spiritual experiences have almost always been expressed in a degree of osmosis with cultures. It has, in fact, often been difficult to differentiate between culture and religion. When we call people Jews it can mean either that they are members of the Jewish race or that they follow the Jewish religion. The same applies to American Indians and to other cultures. The religions of clans, tribes, cities, empires have shared and still share in all social symbolism. At times, this virtual fusion between spirituality and culture has created social systems dominated by the sacred, in which understanding of the divine legitimizes the established order and power. At other times, although society has been shot through with this spiritual culture, it has managed not to succumb to a sacred regime.

Arnold Toynbee was one of the first to insist that the encounter between religion and culture, or 'civility', as he called it, is basic and constitutive.[6] In the anthropology of Émile Durkein, 'religion is the soul of culture'. Cardinal Ratzinger prefers the term 'heart'. On the process of evangelization he wrote: 'If you withdraw from a culture the religion that stems from it as its own, you destroy the culture from its heart. If a new heart (in our case, Christianity) is implanted, it seems inevitable that the organism, unprepared for it, will reject the foreign organ. It is difficult to imagine anything positive in this operation.'[7] Recently, as Pope Benedict XVI, he has decided to amalgamate the Pontifical Secretariat for Inter-religious Dialogue with the Pontifical Secretariat for Culture. No one denies the importance of the two bodies being able to act always in tandem, but there are those who interpret this action as the pope saying that religions as such cannot unite or even dialogue. The most that can be expected would be a coming together of cultures. The Latin-American experience of macro-ecumenism, in which religions meet for dialogue and to profess a joint witness of service to the people, contradicts this institutional pessimism. Above all, I hope that the pope's decision does not contain any insinuation that Islam or any other world religion should be reduced to the more general category of 'culture' – unless Christianity were also no longer to be recognized as a religion but only as simply western culture dressed in what we might call 'Christian spirituality'.

Both because communities and peoples intermingle and because spiritual traditions should help cultures move beyond themselves, all the great religions, while remaining linked to the cultures in which they are embedded, try to be freer and to define themselves as inter-cultural or even universal. Although Pope Benedict XVI seems to think that Christianity and Hellenism are almost synonymous (cf. his Regensburg lecture of 12 Sept. 2006), all the Christian churches consider *catholicity* to be a *nota ecclesiae*.

Islam calls itself universal. A 'mother-of-saint', a priestess of Candomblé, corrected me: I should write that the religion of Orishas is African in origin and not an Afro–Brazilian religion. In fact it is true that many of its adherents are not from Afro culture. And there are Umbanda and Candomblé yards in Spain, Switzerland, and Italy. Even in religions more strongly linked to one culture (e.g., Tibetan Buddhism), evolution over time and the relationship among different cultures have produced a distinction between what was called religion as such and the culture. In some sense, it has been in the West that society has gained the greatest independence from religion. To an extent, secular society became possible by making the distinction between culture and religion. There are even those who think that the concept of 'religion', considered as a specialized institution, is a western invention.[8]

No culture is static: its borders are always intercultural and pluralistic. In the same way, each religion is tied to various cultures and not just to one. Christianity has a Judaic origin, a Semitic soul, but has developed in Hellenic culture. Here we are currently seeking to live a less western Christianity, more Latin American, African, Asiatic, or Oceanic. Buddhism was born in India, but today there are more Buddhists in Japan, Tibet, and China. The number of Muslims of non-Arab origin is growing every day throughout the world. What does this tell us as a challenge to and way forward for the human race?

## III. Diversity, a constituent element of every society

The plurality of cultures, together with the religious pluralism that stems from it, is a reality from which there is no escape. The face of today's world is coming to be a plurality of pluralisms. This is not an inevitable evil with which we are forced to live. On the contrary, it is a divine grace containing a sort of new divine revelation. It is not just a matter of believing that, just as the Bible contains the scriptures of a divine revelation for Jewish and Christian communities, the Koran is the same for Muslims, the Vedas for Hindus, and so forth. It is more than that. It is believing that, as a Christian, I receive a divine revelation of the Word that God has addressed to others as Muslims, Buddhists, or adherents of indigenous or Black traditions. These revelations do indeed tell us something new about God and about ourselves. Not to make us change religion, but to open our faith to the diversity of the divine words given out of love for the human race. It is this theologal dimension of inter-cultural and inter-religious encounter that we can call *hiero-diversity*. This means accepting religious diversity and the authenticity of every spiritual way, not just for those who choose it but for the whole of humankind. So the diversity of spiritual ways is on offer to us not simply as a broad marketplace of religious constructs in which we can live a degree of religious eclecticism, as is common today. The cultural and religious pluralism truly open to hiero-diversity certainly contains a degree of syncretism in the sense that no religious system is isolated and one influences another. Nevertheless, we are at present faced not with a syncretism of blending-in but with a model of multiculturalism that Zigmund Bauman calls 'a cacophony of voices, a confusion, and even an ideology of the end of ideologies'.[9] This multiculturalism overarching cultures is marked by an exacerbated individualism and people's inability to commit to anything.

In a society as complex as ours is more than ever becoming, it is not right to classify people in simplistic fashion according to a single and uniform identity, whether religious or cultural. We can all feel identified, at one and the same time, with the city or country of our birth or where we live, with the religion we belong to, with a philosophical tendency we embrace, with the social class of our origins, with the profession we carry on, with a sexual preference, and so on. Everyone's cultural identity, like that of societies, is becoming increasingly diversified and plural. Previously, the ideal of spirituality common to the classical religions was achieving 'inner unification'. The renunciations common to the way of monks or *sanyasis* were designed for this purpose. Today spiritual wisdom may reside not so much in renunciation as in harmonizing this divine diversity in ourselves, in our religions, and in the world.

Fr Jacques Dupuis put forward a new pneumatic theology: a reflection, that is, on the action of the Holy Spirit in other religions and spiritual traditions, to 'describe how this Spirit reveals more truth and grace to others than the part available to us in the Christian tradition'.[10] A theology of hiero-diversity accepts this revelation made to others and seeks, through them, to learn what new and different things God is saying to us, Christians.

## IV. Challenges to an acceptance of hiero-diversity

Thinking in terms of hiero-diversity means, above all, accepting that our theology and our discourse about God are partial and incomplete. Hiero-diversity calls every kind of totalitarianism of the truth to account, whether it is an official totalitarianism (as still found in certain attitudes and pronouncements of the hierarchy) or a diplomatic and gentlemanly totalitarianism, which can see itself as equally possessing *the* truth.

Some conflicts still going on within each religious confession show the difficulty of accepting the divine presence and actions in the other. The conflicts, even violence, between different groups within Islam, or between Christians of different churches in Kosovo or Northern Ireland, have social and political causes, but the spirituality that should be a factor for peace-making acts rather as incitement to violence when it considers itself master of the truth.

Such conflicts do not occur only in regions such as Iraq or in nations at war. In Brazil and other countries of this continent, the Black population was for centuries forced to accept baptism. This led to many people becoming nominally Catholic or Evangelical but attending Afro rites on the quiet. In the 1980s some priests and priestesses of Candomblé spoke out against this syncretism and condemned the double allegiance. They did so in order to defend Afro culture and to assert their independence of certain sectors of the Catholic hierarchy that refused to accept them. Many people who live this double allegiance carry on not just hiding their belonging to Candomblé from their parents, but also hiding their belonging to the Catholic Church from their 'mother-of-saint'.

Apart from this, some pastors of Pentecostal Churches carry on a veritable crusade against cults of African origin. They also inveigh against Carnival and any 'worldly' cultural manifestation – with the exception of capitalist politics, in which they join 'to spread the kingdom of God'.

At the Fourth Synod of the Italian Church, held in Verona in October 2006, Don Luigi Adami, a worker for ecumenism, declared: 'If we are to achieve inter-religious dialogue, two conversions are necessary: first, renouncing the claim that my vision is complete; second, moving from an attitude of supremacy to a continuous search for truth. Only on the basis of these two conversions will dialogue as a pedagogy of listening be possible.'

## V. Toward a theology and a spirituality of hiero-diversity

Diversity is good because life, as it is, is diversified. According the Convention on Biological Diversity, 'biodiversity' is not only the variety of the living organisms existing on the land, in the air, and in the waters but also the complementarity and relationship among them. Life is formed when various micro-organisms interact and make up a complex network that forms the living body of a plant or animal. In order to live, beings are dependent on the health of their organism but also on a network of life, the 'ecosystem'.

Biodiversity is a new concept for science, but for ages historical cultures have contemplated a unifying principle present in the diversity of living beings. The Xingú Indians say that the spirit of the waters resides in the forest and the spirit of the forest is re-made in the rivers. Afro communities speak of *Axé* as the divine energy present in the most diverse manifestations as source of love and joy.

A theology of hiero-diversity applies the same principle to cultures. No group can live without integration with others. This connection has an anthropologically spiritual dimension. This is a dimension in which culture sees itself not as self-sufficient but as interlinked with others. Religion can then serve as means of making us more human. Hiero-diversity crosses religious communities but also goes beyond religions: it allows us to experience belonging to a faith without becoming enclosed within it.

Furthermore, a theology of hiero-diversity testifies not only that diversity of cultures and religions is a space for divine self-revelation but also that, in this loving relationship of God with an ever more diverse humankind, divinity clothes itself in various guises and takes on, as a divine attribute, not only unity but also diversity. By a new route, the intuition of the ancient apophatic theology is confirmed. God is mystery. As the ancients said, everything we can say about God tells us more about ourselves than about God. We need to overcome the artificiality of classifications that take no account of reality and renounce the Christian tradition's patriarchal analogies for God. This is a great challenge for the religions ever tempted to dogmatism. The Brazilian theologian Faustino Teixeira, in his admirable work on the theology of religions, speaks of the 'singularity of Christianity as a religion of otherness'.[11]

This endeavour implies rooting myself in my own culture but doing so precisely in order to become capable of being what Ernesto Balducci called 'a planetary human being'. This is how he explains it: 'Without denying anything of what I am, I must intuit a new identity as believer. Planetary human beings are post-Christian, in that determinations that divide them from the rest of the human race do not apply to them. [. . .] The New Testament expression that best expresses my faith is the one that appears many times spoken by apostles and prophets in Acts and Revelation: "I am no more than a human being". [. . .] This is my profession of faith, in the shape of hope. Those who call themselves atheists, or secularists, and want a Christian to complete the series of representations on the proscenium of culture need not come looking for me. I am no more than a simple human being.'[12]

*Translated by Paul Burns*

*Notes*

1. Cf. Stefano Allieve, *Pluralismo* (Coll. 'Parole delle Fedi'), Bolgna: EMI, 2006, p. 12.

2. Samuel P. Huntington, *The Clash of Civilizations and the Remaking of the World Order*, New York: Simon & Schuster, 1996.

3. Amartya Sen, *Identità e Violenza*, Rome; Latenza, 2006, p. 4

4. This is the classic definition proposed by Sir Edward Burnett Tylor in *Primitive Culture* (1871), cited by Anna Casella Paltrinieri, *Oltre le Frontiere: Antropologia per avicinare i popoli*, Negarine di S. Pietro in Cariano: Il Segno dei Gabrieli, 2002, p. 38.

5. Joseph Ratzinger, *Fede, Verità, Tolleranza, Cristianesimo e le religione del mondo*, Siena: Cantagalli, 2003, p. 62.

6. Arnold Toynbee, *Civilization on Trial*, Oxford, O.U.P., 1948.

7. Ratzinger, *Fede, Verità, op. cit*, p. 61.

8. Cf. Gwen Griffith-Dickson, 'Religion – A Western Invention?' in *Concilium* 2003/4, pp. 13–21.

9. Zigmunt Bauman, *Comunidade: a Busca per segurança no mundo atual*, Rio de Janeiro: Jorge Zahar, 2003, p. 112.

10. Jacques Dupuis, *Vers une théologie chrétienne du pluralisme religieux*, Paris: Cerf, 1997.

11. Faustino Teixeira, *Teologia das Religiões, Visão Panorâmica*, São Paulo: Paulinas, 1995, pp. 218ff. Available on the internet as an article in *RELaT* at www.servicioskoinonia.org.

12. Ernesto Balducci, *L'Uomo Planetario*, Brescia: Camunia, ¹1985, p. 189.

# Is the Cosmic Christ Greater than Jesus of Nazareth?

LEONARDO BOFF

The process of globalization signifies more than just an economic-financial-media phenomenon; it ushers in a new phase in the history of the earth and of the human race.[1] It is the time when all the tribes can meet each other and exchange knowledge, values, and ethical and spiritual traditions and usher in a dialogue among the most diverse cultures and religions.[2] All systems must inevitably become open and no longer remain closed as they were very largely in the past. Closed systems create their own world-views, their own hierarchy of values, and their own religious truths held to be, as a general rule, unique or at least the best. Today they can no longer be like that. This would be reductionism or lack of acknowledgment of what the Spirit is doing in the history of these peoples.

Humankind has come to realize that we can be human, wise, and religious in the most varied forms. All of these reveal latent potentialities in human beings. In the end, we understand that that we are an infinite project that can be indefinitely expressed and can shape its history down many paths. The one hidden object suited to our desires and our impulse to communicate and love can only be Being. Only thus will we be satisfied.

This new situation poses serious questions for Christianity, especially in regard to the figure of Jesus, believed in and proclaimed as Christ and only Son of God incarnate and the universal saviour. How are we to place the Christian way alongside other spiritual paths and Jesus beside those others seen by their followers also as bearers of grace and salvation?

We have to recognize that Christianity was developed in the cultural context of the Mediterranean world and necessarily shares the limitations of this closed system. It is now being challenged to think its offer in the perspective opened up by globalization and by the unification of the human family, bearing in mind that we are products and expression of a cosmos in evolution, a substrate common to all phenomena.

Christianity is not a fossil petrified in its doctrinal formulations and historical expressions. It has the nature of a living organism that grows and flourishes as all living organisms do – exchanging values and truths while retaining its basic identity. Therefore it has the opportunity of displaying hitherto latent intrinsic qualities, ones that can emerge in interaction with other religions and spiritual figures for the benefit of all humanity, especially that part of it that is suffering most. Christianity should be a good thing for creation and for the human family and not a problem, let alone a nightmare.

## I. Universalist categories of Christianity

Within Christianity there are certain theological categories that allow it to be an open and not a closed system, such as, for example, understanding creation as a form of God's progressive self-manifestation; the kingdom as God's global project for the whole of creation; the offer of salvation as made to all in all times and circumstances (*mysterium salutis*); the Word as 'the true light, which enlightens everyone, [. . .] coming into the world' (John 1.9); the Spirit as filling the universe and being 'the breath of life' (Gen. 6.17; Exod. 37.10–14); the cosmic dimension of Christ as in the letters to the Ephesians and Colossians. This Christian positiveness is, by its nature, universalist and non-exclusive. I want to concentrate on the relevance of the cosmic Christ,[3] as a given in the evolutionary process, so as to relate Jesus of Nazareth to other figures who can also well be expressions of this cosmic Christ.

## II. The risk of a Christian colonialism?

We need, first and foremost, to put aside the temptation to a possible Christian colonialism. We need to pay more attention to content than to words. The content can be present in other religions, although it may be expressed in other words. If we make a special effort to grasp the content beyond the formulations, we shall surely discover surprising convergences.

At the present time we are becoming more and more accustomed to taking the cosmic and biological presuppositions of questions into account, since they are all expressions of a vast evolutionary process still in process.[4] Everything that exists pre-exists in some form. Before appearing in human history, Jesus, Siddhartha Guatama, Chuang Tzu, and others were in gestation within the universe. On account of what they did they were called Christ, in Jesus' case, or Buddha, in Siddhartha Guatama's. All of them have cosmic dimensions to the extent that the entire universe worked to make their appearance possible. What emerged in them did not become a personal monopoly. They gave archetypal shape to potentialities inherent in the universe. So we can say that Jesus emerges as a singular expression of the cosmic Christ. The cosmic Christ does not exhaust all the possible forms of his manifestation in Jesus, a man from the Mediterranean, limited in time and space. Much the same holds for Siddhartha Guatama, who does not exhaust all the potentialities present in Buddha. It would fall to a radical (going to the deepest roots) theology to identify other figures who would qualify as Christ even if they were not called Jesus of Nazareth, or as Buddha even if they were not identified with Siddhartha Guatama.

## III. A Christianity beyond 'Christianity'

Christianity itself takes us to a self-surpassing that avoids exclusivism. There is, for example, a statement by Vatican II that says: 'By his incarnation, he, the Son of God has in a certain way united himself with each individual' (GS 22b). This means: every human being was touched by the Son of God, not just the baptized and Christians. He has to do with all members of the human family, irrespective of their religious adherence. Through being human, we bear Christic dimensions.

The Council of Chalcedon (451) dogmatically professed that Jesus Christ, being God, is 'perfect in humanity, the same truly God and truly man, [. . .] consubstantial with us as regards his humanity, like us in all respects except for sin'. This profession is laden with anthropological significance. Basically, it is saying that what is attributed to Jesus can be attributed to every human being, bearer of the same nature that was formed down billions of years of cosmic history.

In real terms, in him are present all the energies and physical–chemical elements that were forged at the core of the great vermilion stars before they exploded and spread these elements throughout the universe. These elements became part of the formation of the galaxies, the stars, the planets, and our own physicality. The iron that ran in the veins of Jesus or of Siddhartha Guatama, the phosphorus and calcium that strengthened their bones and their nerves, the nitrogen and phosphate that ensured their growth, the 65 per cent oxygen and 18 per cent carbon of which their bodies were composed, made Jesus and Siddhartha Guatama truly cosmic beings.

As the universe has not only exteriority but also interiority, we can say that their psychic depth was inhabited by the most primitive movements of the cosmic unconscious, vegetable, animal, and human, by the most archaic dreams and the most primeval passions, by the deepest archetypes and the most ancient symbols.

In a word, Jesus and Siddhartha Guatama are also products of the great initial explosion and of the developments that followed it. Their roots are to be found in the Milky Way, their cradle in the solar system, their home on planet Earth, and their actual dwelling in Palestine, in a town called Nazareth, for Jesus, and in India, in Pali and Benares, for Siddhartha Guatama.

They are members of the human family. Like all other human beings, they are *animals*, of the mammal *class*, the primate *order*, the hominid *family*, the *genus homo*, the species *sapiens* and *demens*. Jesus and Siddhartha are also sons of the history of humankind, of Israel and of India. Both are representatives of the culture of their times. They thought and acted with the resources these cultures provided for them.

Without these historic-cosmic determinants, they would not be real, as they were. Jesus, for example, would not be the person who walked the dusty tracks of Palestine, proclaiming a new state of consciousness, that we are in fact all sons and daughters of God and workers for a kingdom built on a new relationship with God, called Father and with characteristics of a Mother, in which the core factors were the poor, universal love and companionship, and unconditional forgiveness.

## IV. Two ways of understanding the incarnation

Let us briefly consider the figure of Jesus, since he is of our spiritual household. The Christian faith professes that this man Jesus was contemplated (anointed) to be the incarnate Son of God. It tried to explain this blessed event in two ways. The first starts from the Son who came down with love and sympathy for human nature and took it on. Our humanity began to belong to the Son who was then humanized or made flesh. The other starts from human beings, whose nature is to be an infinite project and capable of total openness to God. Jesus opened himself so radically to the Son that he became identified with him. He knew himself to be Son in calling God Abba-Father of goodness.

Now, if Jesus was divinized in the Son and if the Son was humanized in Jesus and this Jesus is equal to us in all things, this then means that being Son made human and person made divine is within the possibilities of humankind. If it were not, it would be impossible for this blessed event to have occurred. Each one of us, in our own manner but in real and concrete form, is called to the *homo assumptus*: the human being taken up within the mystery of the Son, or else becoming the receptacle of the Son who is seeking to take human form.

## V. 'Christic' and Christian

Pierre Teilhard de Chardin (d. 1955) saw this cosmic insertion of Jesus, called Christ, and coined the term 'Christic' as distinct from Christian.[5] Creation and humankind objectively possess a Christic dimension. This is an objective fact, linked to the mystery of creation in its process of evolution/expansion/self-creation. Now, this objective fact becomes subjective when it reaches the consciousness of the man Jesus and in his followers, who formed and form a community whose destiny revolves around this new state of consciousness. 'Christic' is then changed into 'Christian', which is 'Christic' conscientized, subjectivized, and made history.[6]

This reflection recalls St Augustine, in his response to a pagan philosopher (*Epistola* 102) or in his *Retractationes* (I. 13, 3): 'That which is now given the name of Christian religion always existed beforehand and was not absent from the origin of the human species, until Christ came in the flesh; it was then that the true religion, which already existed, began to be called Christian.'

In other words, the historical Jesus does not exhaust all the possibilities contained in the Christic. The Christic can emerge in other figures. Truth to tell, it comes out in every human person, in all living organisms, in every being in the universe, in matter, in the sub-atomic realm, in the primordial forces.

If we are to understand such statements, we need to clarify the word 'Christ'.[7] This is not a noun but an adjective that is attributed to a person. The Greek *christos* means 'the anointed', and the Hebrew *messiah* also means 'anointed'. 'Anointed' is a term applied to those who are consecrated and assigned to carry out a particular mission.[8] The king, the prophets, the priests were 'anointed', consecrated to fulfil a specific role: the king to govern with righteousness, paying particular attention to the disadvantaged; prophets to proclaim the word; priests to celebrate the sacred rites. But all individuals in their singularity are also 'anointed', since they are called by God by their name and have their place in the divine plan. Jesus was called Christ by reason of the redemptive and liberative work he performed in an exemplary and archetypal manner. Note the following logic: the man Jesus became Christ and the Christ became the *Logos* or Son of God. The Christ thereby became the manifestation of the *Logos* or the Son.

Buddhism has followed a similar course.[9] At the start there was Siddhartha Guatama, the historical being who lived six hundred years before Christ. Through a process of interiorization and ascesis he achieved 'enlightenment', which is a radical immersion in Being. He then began to be called 'Buddha', which means 'the enlightened'. But this enlightenment – being Buddha – is not the monopoly of Siddhartha Guatama. It is offered to all. There is, therefore, 'Buddhahood', that transcendent Reality which can communicate itself in many ways in our human history. The Buddha is a manifestation of 'Buddhahood', which is the purest light, the divine light and the unnameable essence.

As will be seen, the actual content of 'Christ' or 'Buddha' refers to the same Reality. Both reveal God. Siddhartha Guatama is a manifestation of the cosmic Christ in the same way as Jesus of Nazareth. Or Jesus of Nazareth is an 'Enlightened One', like Buddha. Both were 'anointed' for this mission.

Taoism says something similar. As the master Chuang Tzu says, 'There is no place where the Tao cannot be found. . . . It is great in everything, complete in everything, universal in everything, integral in everything'.[10] Tao is the universal Way, the cosmic Order, the supreme Force, the ultimate Mystery. Every being (person, animal, stone) possesses its Tao, meaning that it carries it in a particular form and so reveals it. By uniting ourselves with the cosmic Tao, we nourish the Tao that is in us and immerse ourselves deeper in it.

## VI. Other figures of the 'cosmic Christ' in history

As individual expressions of the cosmic Christ or of the Enlightenment or of the Tao, each in his or her own manner and form, we might point to figures such as Krishna, Francis of Assisi, Mahatma Gandhi, or Pope John XXIII, Bishop Helder Câmara, Martin Luther King, Jr., Mother Teresa of Calcutta, to choose a few from among so many. And these by no means exhaust the possibilities of this sublime Reality. It is present in all of us. But in them it gathered strength to such a degree that they have become reference points and guiding archetypes for millions of human beings who also discover themselves to be children of God and to share in Enlightenment or the Tao.

Another expression of the cosmic Christ that escapes the 'Christianization' of the subject is the expression Wisdom, or *Sophia*.[11] This is present in all peoples that have produced teachers and wise men and women. They exalt Wisdom as moulding life and the universe into its most harmonious form.

The Old Testament dedicates a whole book – Wisdom of Solomon – to this figure, in which it is stated that all thing were created through her: 'Although she is but one, she can do all things, and while remaining in herself, she renews all things . . . She reaches mightily from one end of the earth to the other, and she orders all things well' (7.27; 8.1). This Wisdom passes through the world promoting integrity, balance, splendour, and beauty. Every being in the universe is the fruit of Wisdom and is her sacrament. She is another expression of the cosmic Christ, of Buddhahood, and of the Tao.

*Logos* is another category used by St John and the first Christian theologians to show the universality of the cosmic Christ. However complex the many meanings of *Logos* might be,[12] its essential nucleus seeks to express the power of intelligibility and ordering in the universe, which could not remain as an impersonal force but had to possess the highest degree of subjective being and understanding.

The well-known Brazilian Yoga master Hermógenes has, without falling into facile syncretism but based on a very deep spiritual experience of union with the Whole, produced this formula, which he calls 'Glory to the One':[13]

I asked a blessing from Krishna
and it was Christ who blessed me.
I prayed to Christ
and it was Buddha who heard me.
I called on Buddha
and it was Krishna who answered me.

*Translated by Paul Burns*

## Notes

1. L. Boff, *A civilização planetária*, Rio de Janeiro: Sextante, 2003.
2. A brief bibliography on the subject: J. Dupuis, *Toward a Christian Theology of Religious Pluralism*, Maryknoll, NY: Orbis, 1997; J. Hick, *God Has Many Names*, Philadelphia: Westminster, 1982; P. Knitter, *Introducing the Theology of Religions*, Maryknoll, NY: Orbis, 2002; C. J. Pieris Lopes, *Pluralismo teológico e cristologia*, Petrópolis: Vozes, 2005; F. de Mier, *Salvados y salvadores. Teología de la salvación para el hombre de hoy*, Madrid: San Pablo, 1998; J. M. Vigil,

*Teología del pluralismo teológico*, Quito: Abya Yala, 2005; F. Teixeira, *Teologia das religiões*, São Paulo: Paulinas, 1995; A. Pieris, *El rostro asiático de Cristo*, Salamanca: Sígueme, 1991.

3. Cf. L. Boff, *O evangelho do Cristo cósmico*, Rio de Janeiro: Record, 2006; A. D. Galloway, *The Cosmic Christ*, London: Nisbet, 1951; H. Wells, *The Christic Center. Life-Giving and Liberating*, Maryknoll, NY: Orbis, 2004; D. Edwards, *Jesus and the Cosmos*, Mahwah, NJ: Paulist, 1991; G. Schiwy, *Der cosmische Christus*, Munich: Kösel, 1990; J. Moltmann, 'Der kosmische Christus', in *idem, Wer ist Christus für uns heute*, Gütersloh: Gütersloher, 1994, ch. 6; J. Dupuis, 'The Cosmic Christ of Our First Parents', in *Toward a Christian Theology, op. cit.* pp. 83–122; H. J. Gabathuler, *Jesus Christus Haupt der Kirche – Haupt der Welt*, Zürich & Stuttgart, 1965; J. Ernst, *Pleroma und Pleroma Christi*, Regensburg: Pustet, 1970; R. Nooth, 'The Scotist Cosmic Christ', in *De doctrina Johannis Duns Scotus*, vol. 3, Rome, 1968, pp. 169–217; J. A. Merino Abad, 'Cristología escotista y creación', in *Carthaginensia* 25 (1998), pp. 101–16.

4. B. Swimme and T. Berry, *The Universe Story*, San Francisco: Harper, 1992.

5. Cf. collection of the main texts in L. Boff, *O evangelho do Cristo cósmico, op. cit.*, pp. 35–7.

6. See n. 3 above.

7. Cf. A. Orbe, 'La unción del Verbo', in *Analecta Gregoriana* 113 (1961), pp. 67–71.

8. Cf. the commentaries by J.-Y. Leloup and L. Boff, *Terapeutas do deserto*, Petrópolis: Vozes, 1997, pp. 148–51; see also C. G. Jung, *Jesus, archetypisch gesehen* (in complete works, vol. 11), Olten: Walter, 1971.

9. See n. 6 above.

10. See *The Way of Chuang Tzu*, trans. Thomas Merton, New York, NY: New Directions, 1979; n.e. London: Burns & Oates, 2003..

11. Cf. D. Edwards, *Jesus the Wisdom of God. An ecological theology*, Maryknoll, NY: Orbis, 1995; A. Feuillet, *Le Christ. Sagesse de Dieu d'après les Epîtres pauliniennes*, Paris: Beauchesne, 1966.

12. A detailed discussion of the various meanings of *Logos* can be found in Dupuis, *Toward a Christian Theology, op. cit.*, pp. 83–113.

13. *Cancão Universal*, Rio de Janeiro: Record, 1991, p. 47.

# Mediation and Opacity of Scriptures and Dogmas

JAVIER MELLONI

## I. The function of sacred texts

All belief systems feature a certain number of central texts that narrate the events on which their specific traditions are based. These accounts, which take an oral form initially and are committed to writing at a later date, enable a faith community to understand itself. The sacred texts represent both a conclusion and a starting point. They are a conclusion because, even though they refer back to the origins, they were written down much later than the episodes they describe. They are events that have been interpreted and theologized at a particular moment, which requires a process of maturation and of self-understanding of faith. They are established as sacred scriptures which, from that point on, become an ineluctable standard of reference for subsequent generations, and continue to act as guides for those seeking new horizons of meaning.

The biblical narratives gather together the foundational experiences of Judaeo-Christian tradition, which comprises two passovers, in the form of two transitions or passages: the Old Testament is centred upon the experience of a people freed from slavery, in which God takes the initiative in favour of an oppressed group with which he enters into a covenantal alliance, whereas the New Testament essentially revolves around the transcendence of the death of Jesus of Nazareth. In both instances we are concerned with an experience of liberation, and in each case this is conceived of as an irruption of the divine into history. The Old Testament is much more concerned with an intra-historical and collective liberation, whereas the New Testament emphasizes the trans-historical and personal aspect of this liberation, while radicalizing faith in a God who involves himself in human affairs, all the way to the representation of Jesus as God's complete and definitive self-bestowal.

The Sinaitic Covenant and the Paschal event are two epicentres from which, so to speak, concentric waves of narrative and doctrine move out. All God's other manifestations are to be interpreted in the light of these key moments. In both cases, faith matures by means of a process in which the exclusive nature of this event is affirmed to the advantage of one's own group (Exod. 15; 23.20-33; Deut. 7.1–8; 26.8–19), or the affirmation of Christ's unique mediation (John 1.18; 14.6; Acts 4.12; 1 Tim. 2.5) opens up horizons of greater universality. Nevertheless, this process is not always evident in the texts, in which passages from very different eras and situations appear side-by-side, and simultaneously allow and disallow this interpretation: the universalist readings of second and third Isaiah (Isa. 40–55; 56–66) contrast with the highly nation-specific books of the Maccabees at a time when Jewish identity was at stake. Treating the books without distinction as the word of God – 'All scripture is inspired by God' (2 Tim. 3.16) – hinders the process of distinguishing the essential from the circumstantial. The biblical corpus was established as canonical at times when identity was threatened. The initial delimitation of the Old Testament occurred after the return from exile in the fifth century BC, and the second, definitive adjustment took place between the second and fourth centuries AD, at a time when the Jewish community, expelled from its homeland, had to demarcate itself both from Hellenic culture and from Christians. This meant rejecting the more Hellenistic texts, which had been accepted for a time as sharing in biblical revelation. Two criteria of choice were clearly operative: only those texts were retained that had been written in Hebrew and in the land of Israel.[1] The canon of the New Testament was also established through complex processes that that led to discrimination between certain texts and others. Uncertainties persisted up to the time of the Reformation, which, with regard to the Old Testament, finally adopted the restricted Hebrew canon.

Once accepted as the *Word of God* – as they are proclaimed in liturgical celebrations – the sacred texts define an extremely dense area of revelation, but at the risk of setting this apart. By narrating historical events of a specific nation, interpreted by the very same nation, they run the risk of reducing their content to the literalism of a specific history, thereby losing their universality. That is the basis of the strength and limitation of the linear and historicist biblical paradigm: its effectiveness is rooted in its specificity but it then has difficulty in raising itself to a symbolic level on which it could acknowledge other interventions of God in other historical developments. The linearity of one's own history can prevent acknowledgement of the fact that there are also paschal rhythms (a sequence of deaths and resurrections) that also occur in the *salvation history* of other peoples and traditions.

Biblical exclusiveness passed to Christianity around the unique figure of Jesus the Messiah because of this linear historicist mentality. This influences the dogmas and theological systems to which this kind of exclusiveness gives rise.

## II. Meaning of dogmas and of theological systems

Dogmas involve a leap from narrative to concept. Narration, in spite of its specificity, contains an excess of symbolic significance, which the concept encloses. We need conceptual language, to be sure, in order to probe various possible implications, but while remaining aware that everything that we can say about God is only analogical. *Ana-logy*, insofar as it means a word that is proportionate to a higher, superior, or transcendent reality, reminds us that all human discourse is subject to radical inadequacy before God, whether conceived as Ultimate Reality or as a personal Being, but as one that cannot be reduced to a human scale. Nevertheless, we cannot avoid referring to Him – or Her – on the basis of our conception of what is human, which is always culturally and historically conditioned.

Using words to refer to Mystery is a human necessity that we may legitimately exercise only if we understand – and reverence – the fact that any approximation to the sphere of the divine will always be a reduction, a diminution of something so disproportionate to us that we are unable to encompass it. Its relevance is grounded in the *symbolic* potential which it contains. I refer here to *symbol* in its original acceptation as the phenomenal expression of something essentially other (from the Greek *sumbolon* = *sun* + *ballein*): to its capacity to conjoin different spheres, such as the visible and the invisible, the tangible and the intangible, the conceivable and the revealed, the confirmed and the hoped for. This conjunction, which simultaneously conceals and reveals, is neither static nor univocal but is beset with a permanent deprivation. Theological discourse about Mystery approaches it to the extent that it is transcended. That is the paradox we have to bear with: we require certain words but are then led by them to what is beyond their reach.

The great difficulty with dogmas is that they use a human language – which is always culturally and historically conditioned – to refer to a transhuman reality. That does not mean that they indicate nothing; they do: hence the importance of ecclesial discernment, the *sensus fidelium*, for discovering the most appropriate formulation. Dogma comes from *doceo*, which has a dual meaning: on the one hand, 'believe', 'think' (in the sense of 'opine), and on the other hand, 'decide', 'decree'. This gave rise to the two meanings that it had in classical Antiquity: in philosophical circles it referred to an opinion held by a philosopher or school of philosophy, whereas in political circles it would signify an order or decree handed down by legitimate authority. It occurs in the Acts of the Apostles with reference to the decisions adopted by the apostles assembled in the Council of Jerusalem.[2] The Christian meaning of *dogma* includes elements of both meanings. When it leans toward the legal side and is understood as a decree, its legitimacy is distorted, because dogma should be understood only as a 'glimpse', as a 'direction to follow'. We need these formulations of faith insofar as they guide faith in a specific direction, but on condition that their epistemological status is interpreted correctly.

It is a matter of the 'Do not hold on to me' (John 20.17a) that Jesus addressed to Mary Magdalen after the resurrection. This warning should apply to all dogmas and theological systems: none of them can encompass the Mystery of God, for they are merely indicative. They are indicative in the sense of what Jesus then says to Mary Magdalen: '. . . go to my brothers and say to them, "I am ascending to my Father and your Father, to my God and your God"' (John 20.17b). From that point Jesus is *ascending*, and we are all included in this *ascent*. Therefore we are completing the Body of Christ formed by humankind, the achievement whose fullness is everyone's task.[3] However, the Body of Christ is the Christian term used to refer to the manifest reality of God, of the world, and of humankind, which, according to the Christian approximation, come together in Christ Jesus. But if it is a joint task, we have to allow our brothers and sisters – other religious traditions – to communicate their experiences and glimpses of fullness in their own words, and ensure that our words, together with theirs, may *ascend* and reach fulfilment.

## III. Idols and icons

We can understand dogmas adequately only if we are aware of their radical precariousness and inadequacy. They point to a mystical dimension, and when we speak of mysticism we are not justifying the incoherent obfuscation of unverifiable and confused discourse, but appealing for awareness that all human words about God are forms of babbling, radically inadequate approximations sustained only in the silent contemplation of worship and awe and the adequacy of which is demonstrated by their capacity to transform what is human.

Dogmas may be icons or idols. In Greek both words, *eikon* and *eidos,* mean 'image'. Idols are inflated images that point to themselves and distort the process of transcendence. Biblical tradition condemns the worship of idols, to the extent of punishing its practice with a death sentence.[4] Certainly, worship of an idol is tantamount to the destruction of truly effective feeling and thinking. Whereas idols are obstructive, icons disclose. They are passageways, openings of significance with minimal characteristics of their own and the maximum significance allowing a transition through them to increasingly profound and translucent spheres. This is precisely what happens with the dogmas of every tradition: they may be experienced as icons or as idols. It all depends on how they are used.

Words, symbols, and concepts are bearers of psychic energy. They hold the mental energy that we put into them. But they also imprison it. We think inside a system, which also encloses us in itself. Religions, taken as constellations of texts, precepts, rites, and theological developments, form veritable *semiotic cathedrals*. But these same cathedrals can become prisons, depending on the particular epistemological value attributed to their signs and symbols.

This does not mean that we should abolish dogmas, since we need them to indicate different ways ahead, but in full awareness that they are intended to point to a moon that is far beyond the reach of any finger. Ultimately, theological discourse does not pronounce words *about* God, but *from* God and from the human. Theological discourse does not turn God into the object of its discourse but becomes a receptacle of God speaking in it. In the fourth century AD, in the barrenness of the desert, Evagrius Ponticus maintained that 'if you would be a theologian, speak of truth, and if you speak of truth, you will be a theologian'.[5] We need to return to this conceptual desert, which is a place where we are stripped bare but also a place of encounter and renewal. Theologal talk about God is characterized by its radical openness and provisionality. It speaks, and in speaking evokes and convokes, but then withdraws so that revelation may burgeon in Silence.

## IV. Faith and beliefs, *noesis* and *noemas*

One of the opportunities afforded by inter-religious dialogue consists in helping to increase awareness of the theological, anthropological, and cosmological presuppositions that support our own beliefs. When we engage in dialogue with other religions, we do not accede to other conceptions (and symbols) of God on a totally neutral basis, but on the basis of our own conceptions (and symbols). The question is one of thinking and discerning how far we can pierce through the carapace of language and reach the core of faith, so that it becomes accessible and comprehensible for other conceptions of the divine, of the human, and of the world, in the hope of attaining to a sphere that is common to and comprehensible for all humankind. Accordingly, we make a fundamental distinction between faith and belief, in the sense that faith refers to the act of trust in and giving to God (*fides qua*), whereas beliefs are the specific contents of that faith (*fides quae*).[6] To some extent they are inseparable, but they can be distinguished from each other. Faith refers to the integral energy – physical, mental, spiritual – with which we commit ourselves to and involve ourselves in a specific cause or way of life. Beliefs, on the other hand, are mental references we receive from our environment and which we can compare with other models of belief.

Husserl's phenomenology helps us to understand the difficulty of escaping from our own categories in order to grasp others. Our approximation to reality is based on a correlation between an intentional act (*noesis*) and the contents of that act (*noemas*). This means that the content of what we conceive and, therefore, think is intrinsically related to the intentional act by means of which we conceive something: 'Every region and every category of presumed objects is matched phenomenologically not only by a fundamental mode of meanings or propositions, but also by a fundamental mode of originally determinative consciousness of such meanings which is accompanied by a fundamental kind of original evidence'.[7] This makes it impossible to understand the thrust of a particular religious experience from outside. Every religious tradition is an approximation to reality and organizes its contents accordingly. Theological systems are organizations of these *noemas*, which constantly take for granted the substantial and absolute nature of what they have to say about God, without taking sufficient account of the fact that God is treated inside that system as an *object*, which is being assimilated within certain specific categories determined by the perspective that produced this objectification. They do not take sufficient account of the fact that this objectification is already a cognitive limitation provided by the viewpoint of the intentional act (*noesis*). This leaves theology and any theological system unprotected, by stripping them of their absolutist affirmations.

But what they lose in security they gain in openness and availability. Inter-religious dialogue tends to a realization that religion is an approximation, that is, a conception of God from a certain perspective determined by a particular angle of approach.

# V. The threefold decentralization that all religion provides

What is actually at stake in religions is not only their formulations concerning Ultimate Reality; what is essentially characteristic of the religious dimension is its salvific aspect, taking salvation in the broadest sense of the word and in accordance with the various emphases it is given in each tradition: redemption, liberation, enlightenment . . . , in short, its capacity for revealing ways to the fullness of human life. The importance of Christian dogmas and of the various theological systems derived from them does not depend essentially on the brilliance or subtlety of what they affirm, but on their capacity to enlighten human life. Their validity depends on their ability to convey salvation. That is the nature of true orthodoxy: to cast light on right attitudes and actions with regard to life, which makes it become orthopraxis.

Christian dogmas derive from the life of Jesus, from the quality and profundity of his existence and from the fruitfulness of his actions. 'Whoever has seen me has seen the Father' (John 14.9). Truth and Life are united in Jesus. True orthodoxy is that which leads us to live as he lived: becoming ever more Godlike for others. Christian dogmas have to do with one single thing: indicating the mystery of why this conjoining takes place in Christ. This process of explication took place gradually, developing over more than four centuries until the definition of the Christological formulas of the Council of Chalcedon, stating that Christ is wholly God and wholly human, meaning that in him the divine has become entirely integrated with the human and the human with the divine by means of one and the same act: that of giving. If dogmas do not conduce to self-bestowal, they fail to carry out their function.

All this does not imply an exclusivist but a radically open development. Faith in Jesus does not limit encounters with other religious traditions, but quite the contrary: it supposes the surpassing of all limits. Jesus died sent outside the walls of Jerusalem, the messianic city *par excellence*, illustrating the tendency of human beings to bring God down to the level of the categories that we project onto him. The dynamism of faith, which is the paschal dynamism, is a continual process of death and resurrection of our categories regarding God and regarding his ways of showing and revealing himself. Texts, dogmas, and systems are enclosures overflowing with their own contents. Ultimately, they all speak of one and the same thing, which will not allow them to remain closed in on themsleves: that God is revealed precisely in the movement of self-emptying. Christ Jesus is the very icon of this dual emptying of the divine into the human and of the human into the divine, in order make it not a mode of exclusivity but one of discernment: where giving takes place the divine is revealed, and the ultimate Reality that makes all things exist is manifest. This bestowal is the sign of the proclamation of the Word of God which enlightens the life of us humans, whatever the form taken by the specific account which conveys it.

*Translated by J. G. Cumming*

## Notes

1. The following books were rejected: Tobit, Judith, the Additions to the Book of Esther, the Wisdom of Solomon, Ecclesiasticus, Baruch, the Letter of Jeremiah, the Additions to the Book of Daniel, 1 and 2 Maccabees, 3 Maccabees, 3 Esdras, and the Prayer of Manasseh. Thus, the Hebrew canon was reduced to the five books of the Pentateuch, the eight books of the Prophets, and eleven historical or hagiographical books.
2. Cf. Acts 15.22, 25, 28; 16.24.
3. Cf. 1 Cor. 12.27; Eph. 4.12-13.
4. Cf. Exod. 22,19; Deut. 13.7–16; 17.3–7.
5. *On Prayer*, 61.
6. Cf. R. Aubert, *Le problème de l'acte de foi*, Louvain, 1958; Jean Mouroux, *Je crois en Toi: La Rencontre avec le Dieu Vivant*, Paris, 1948; Raymund Panikkar, *The Experience of God: Icons of the Mystery*, Minneapolis, 2006, pp. 24–7.
7. Edmund Husserl, *Ideen zu einer reinen Phänomenologie und phänomenologischen Philosophie: Gesammelte Werke*, Vol. III/1, Book 1, The Hague, 1976, p. 321.

# Mystery in Earthenware Vessels: the Fragmenting of Images of God within New Experiences of Religion

LIEVE TROCH

Leave this chanting and singing and telling of beads!
Whom dost thou worship in this lonely dark corner of a temple with doors
    all shut?
Open thine eyes and see thy God is not before thee!
He is there where the tiller is tilling the hard ground
and where the pathmaker is breaking stones.
He is with them in sun and in shower,
and his garment is covered with dust.
Put off thy holy mantle and even like him come down on the dusty soil!
. . .
Come out of thy meditations and leave aside thy flowers and incense!
What harm is there if thy clothes become tattered and stained?
Meet him and stand by him in toil and in sweat of thy brow.

(from *Gitanjali*, by Rabindranath Tagore)

I watched a woman on a tea–plantation carefully handling two earthen-ware pots and about three litres of water that had to be drawn more than three miles away every morning. The water was ingeniously recycled throughout the day using these two vessels. It was all used to the very last drop to make tea, cook meals, wash, and clean the hut. Where water is scarce, vessels are important, but their economic use to make sure that the full potential of the water is retained as long as possible is especially important. The next day, she had to make the long journey to fetch water all over again.

(Lieve Troch)

Many believers inside and outside traditional Christianity are now aware of a plurality of religions. This awareness, coupled with the existing political and social situation, has produced not only religious tolerance but a profound conviction that the truth is to be reached on a basis much broader than that of one's own denomination alone. Yet a pluralist outlook on life is far from a matter of course for followers of the monotheistic religions. One challenge that theologians working within a pluralist concept have to face is reconsideration of the place of the divine. This article is principally concerned with the location and occasion of the divine in this new context of different religious identities and religious practices.

Although some kind of iconoclasm is a feature of a number of religions, cosmic and meta-cosmic religions locate the divine in narratives, in reflection on tradition and memory, and in rites and interpretations. All religions offer not only definitions, that is, a schematization of the divine, but associated internal arrangements that seek to protect the divine permanently from any form of co-option. Most religions, moreover, usually recognize images and concepts as ways of referring to God, to experience with the divine, and not as God himself ('Let God be God').

Broadly speaking, at present we may distinguish three epistemological areas where pluralism inquires into typical specific religious definitions: the obvious pluralistic space of normal society; the involuntary pluralistic sphere of a refugee or migrant; and the artificially created space of inter-religious dialogue. In this article I shall concentrate on the first and second of these spheres.

## I. Pluralism and the transformation of religions

Pluralism as a religious way of life is a new phenomenon in certain parts of the world. In Asian countries such as Japan, India, Sri Lanka, and Korea confrontation with various forms of religion and spirituality has been a self-evident part of everyday life for a long time now. Men and women adopt different viewpoints with consequences even for institutional religions. They extend from syncretism as a hybrid form of different types of worship and spirituality to a synthesis giving rise to a new kind of faith that transcends and negates the original forms of religion. Asian theologians have already been discussing pluralism for decades. The recent growing attention paid to a theology of the pluralism of faiths in the West is more a result of the changing function, form, and place of religions in western societies, and a consequence of globalization and of migration because of war or the economic situation.

Religion might seem to be disappearing, but it resurfaces in other forms. Believers experiment with new religious experience, in the midst of agnosticism and emphatically atheistic positions and attitudes.

A number of fundamental developments continually lead to changes in relations within the pluralist situation:

1. In western countries, the Christian religion has undergone a fundamental change inasmuch as the secularization process has brought about the departure of a distant and alien God who occupied a particular space. Talking about God has become something that is no longer self-evident, and religion has also undergone a functional change in society.
2. New epistemological processes within religions result in critical approaches to the image of God, unilateral creation of tradition, image-making, rites, and so on. Black, feminist, and indigenous theologies indicate new locations for theology and redefine the relation between the sacred and the profane, the transcendent and the immanent.
3. The everyday, and on occasion emphatic, presence of other religions apart from Christianity demands reflection. On the one hand it leads to a transformation of the traditional exclusive monotheistic notion of God in the direction of a greater degree of openness, and on the other hand in many places it results in a growing fundamentalism.
4. Contacts with several forms of spirituality and worship encourage many people to experiment and change course in their own lives. Some people cobble together their own religious practice. The divine has a number of different faces, but also different faces and aspects in a single human life.

In some countries such as the Netherlands, for example, all this leads to strained relations between an explicitly agnostic society and a partly very devout Islam. In this context inter-religious groups are formed that try to break through the climate of hostility and overcome fundamentalism.

## II. The divine in earthenware vessels. The relativity of images and the importance of images

Aloysius Pieris, the Asian Buddhist scholar and Christian theologian, refers to three levels in every religion: the current appearance of religion in practices and rites; the history and solidified memory of tradition; and the primordial experiences in which these elements originated. In the direct confrontation and dialogue of believers with one another the first contact is generally at the level of rites and practices. Penetration to deeper levels, encounter with one another there, and understanding of and respect for everyone's identity and distinctive features are not easy tasks for believers and theologians.

The plurality of religions leads to fundamentalism or to the acknowledgement of the fragility and limited nature of all discourse about the divine. In the latter case, the metaphor of earthenware vessels as a means of portraying the divine can help to relativize absolute claims. In her book *Ordinarily Sacred*, Lynda Sexson refers to the fact that in religions vessels and boxes have always been important attributes in religious rites. They hold the mysteries and relate to primordial experiences. Vessels and boxes divide two areas, the immediately perceptible and the space within. The 'usefulness' of vessels depends on the empty piece, and on those who can make use of these vessels.

Earthenware vessels are interesting objects. They are familiar in many forms: as everyday utensils; as objects for contemplation in museums; and, in the shape of ancient shards, as challenges for archaeologists and anthropologists, since the domestic arrangements and the economy of a certain period in the past can be inferred from them. Vessels and shards are memorials of the original economy, the primordial experience. Shards provide elements of contexts for the interpretation of earlier economies. The same is true of the shards and vessels of religions: they are the language of the socio-economic reality that was legitimized or challenged by the religion. They are neither value-free nor neutral spaces: religion operates within power relations, and within just and unjust relations, and it legitimizes or challenges. Different denominations feature socio-economic arrangements within which images of God function. These are examined critically, and many vessels are smashed because they are faulty and useless. Analyses by Black, feminist, and socio-economically disadvantaged groups have studied several religions in order to discover how images of the divine contribute to exclusion and marginalization. The combination of shards and present-day vessels constitutes a challenge to theologians to analyze and interpret socio-economic religious relations and possibly to allow a transformation of relations to occur. The demand for a transformation of injustice and deficiencies is part of the primordial experience of religions.

Imagining the divine, God, without flesh and blood, without the body of a community, along with its traditions and wishes, is a bloodless abstraction.

Therefore the new fragmented talk about God in a pluralist society will emanate from traditions and communities that recognize each other in a joint project. Talking about God is primarily saying what the 'presence' of the divine means and brings about.

Where are the epistemological areas in a pluralistic world that lead to 'transformation' and are capable of giving rise to new images of the divine?

## III. The third magisterium

Pieris refers to three spheres where 'revelation' and 'authoritative discourse about the divine' come about: he distinguishes three forms of magisterium. After the first magisterium of the leadership of Christian churches, he describes a second magisterium: that of western theologians and scholars who deal with diversity by way of discussions of exclusivism, inclusivism, and the theology of pluralism. The interaction of the first and second magisteria is a delicate matter, as is shown by the constant clashes between theologians and church leaders. In ecumenical organizations such as the World Council of Churches, where these magisteria are closely involved with one another, decades of dialogue have led to very little change in talk about God and the power relations that emerge in that discourse. The influence of the separate churches on each other brings about scarcely any innovative discourse within their own communities. New theologies arising from subjects that were not discussed for hundreds of years have little influence on official theology. Hopeful developments with regard to the way in which the Christian religion creates openness conducive to pluralistic thinking and behaviour are not immediately apparent.

Pieris argues in favour of a third magisterium. This third magisterium occurs in what he describes as 'basic human communities': places where members of different religions can engage in co-operative action and discussion with non-believers for the liberation of marginalized people and the transformation of relations. Religious identity does not play a primary role in these basic human communities, and dialogue about religion is not a goal in itself. The uniqueness of each contribution is evident in the efforts made to achieve that form of liberation which brings about a transformation of communal life. These communities are *loci theologiae*, places of revelation where authoritative talk about the divine can occur in new forms. The third magisterium touches on a metaphor that Elisabeth Schüssler Fiorenza has made use of: that of a discipleship of equals: a community of equally entitled people seeking to overcome the restrictions of religion, race, class, gender, and culture and their 'exclusivist' effects without taking differences into account. This discipleship of equals is the place where liberating, oppressive, and exclusivist mechanisms in societies are named, evaluated, and transformed in a continual struggle for equality, with respect for each person's identity and diversity.

This discursive praxis, the actual location of the third magisterium, appears in the works of both authors as a pluralistic sphere enjoying a decisive authority with regard to discourse about the divine, though without any uniform definition of it. After all, there is no reason why many different religious narratives cannot all be true. The conclusive criterion is whether this sphere of difference becomes a productive workplace for changing injustice into justice, and poverty and exclusion into equality. Then that location is a magisterium, a decisive instance of revelation of the divine in the midst of plurality.

Neither syncretism nor synthesis is the means by which this location is created and operates. Pieris speaks of a symbiosis in which different religions contribute their own uniqueness in the course of cooperative effort, and open up their own historical memory to one another.

These locations may be places of study combined with practice[1], or places where symbiosis occurs and theologians can also get to work. Talk and action within this third magisterium seem to me to constitute the most challenging instance of renewed discourse about the divine at the present time

Where are we likely to find these places where the third magisterium can prevail? The following are a few examples.

### (a) The shared space of the mountain

There is a uniquely interesting mountain in the centre of Sri Lanka. Different denominations have given it various names, but it is best known as Adam's Peak.

The four religions on the island, Buddhist, Hindu, Muslim, and Christian, recognize this mountain as a sacred eminence. The aboriginal inhabitants of Sri Lanka, the Veddahs, prefer to treat the mountain as a place of worship. Members of the different religions frequent this pluralist location every day, and especially during the religious festivals of one of the four denominations. On Poya Day in particular, when there is a full moon, the mountain is covered with pilgrims who ascend and descend the same path as they make their pilgrimage in a meditative atmosphere. There is scarcely any organization; it is a place for spiritual walking. There are no ritual areas and the mountain is not exclusively occupied by one particular religion. People making their way up and down wish each other the best, and exchange mutual blessings. Unfortunately more and more western tourists are discovering this site, which threatens to alter its religious pluralist character.

## (b) Transgression in a celebration of hope

Like many slums in Asia, those of Colombo in Sri Lanka feature a great variety of cultures, religions, and ethnic groups. The odour of poverty is the same for everyone, and the normal conflicts and mechanisms of exclusion are less pronounced here than in society outside the slums. To my astonishment, during the preparations for the feast of St Sebastian, which is always celebrated exuberantly in the slums, I saw Muslims diligently cleaning the images of the saint with complete dedication in the many niches at street corners. During a celebration of the Eucharist in honour of this saint in the muddy streets, Muslims and Hindus kept the lighting equipment and sound installation continually up to the mark. The pluralist community is mobilized for religious celebrations. This participation is more than taking part in a 'cultural' event, which certain theologians or prominent churchmen and churchwomen allege in their own defence. Muslims do not venerate St Sebastian, and they are not allowed to enter a Catholic church. But in the pluralist community a communal celebration takes place within a specific religious context in order to transform the banality and dreariness of everyday life, and in order to allow some access to hope in reality.

## (c) Symbiosis as a force for transformation in a pluralistic praxis

A group of women, friends and feminists, in Colombo, who are Muslims, Buddhists, Hindus, and Christians, have been working together for some years now in order to improve the position of widows in the culture. Widows are marginalized by taboos at various public events. This exclusion is additionally legitimized by the patriarchal characteristics of the different religions. In a country with some tens of thousands of widows as a result of many years of internal conflicts, these feminists are working to influence the media, establish small businesses with widows, and critically examine practices within the different religions that legitimize oppression. On the occasion of a discussion with western Christian theologians, these women challenged the theologians to consider such actions as forms of interreligious dialogue.

I shall call these three exemplary spaces, theologically speaking, magisteria and sacred ground. These are places where the divine as transforming power is moulded in new vessels of clay. The divine is not called by name explicitly. It is experienced on the mountain. It is lived in a ritual during a specifically religious festival that is capable of transcending dejection and of mobilizing diversity. It is created in the transforming actions of pluralist religious groups.

There are also involuntarily pluralistic situations. Many migrants migrate as a result of war, political situations, or poverty and uprootedness. The no-man's-land, frontiers and borderlands, where they end up existentially and materially, demand considerable inventiveness in order to deal with cultural, linguistic, and religious differences. These locations become either breeding-grounds of fundamentalism or the healing areas of a third magisterium. Other images of the divine can be rendered visible in the borderlands and in no-man's-land. It is a pre-condition that the transformative movement opposing the negative effects of globalization should be driven by these migrants, together with people who choose to live in these borderlands where it is possible to pursue the transformation of socio-economic structures.

The abovementioned pluralistic areas are possibly more interesting for theologians than the sometimes artificially created areas for inter-religious dialogue or scholarly pluralist discourse, for they are places where 'religio' predominates, and 'connections' are made.

What images of God are possible in these multifarious situations and symbiotic areas?

## IV. God in the disruptive moments of history and in daily life.

Religion comes into its own in border situations, where compassion, like equilibrium, is a basic requirement and relations have to be forged anew. It is there that exclusive limits and conflicts between male and female, and between white and black, as well as economic, cultural, and religious differences of opinion, can undergo the effects of liberating relationships. Religion is reborn wherever 'lovers' are to be found and loving relationships are entered into. That is where the new language about God originates, because there precisely the reign of God is established.

The black theologian Delores Williams puts the biblical character of Hagar at the centre of her work about 'Godtalk'. The Egyptian slave-girl Hagar had come from another culture, another religion, and another ethnic background. Her life of drudgery with Abraham and Sarah was her only role and situation in the dominant sphere to which she had been transferred. Hagar is despatched to the desert by Abraham and Sarah as soon as she is no longer of any use to these 'pious' forerunners of present-day religion, and both of them are strong enough to manage for themselves. Hagar struggles to survive in the empty space of the desert, which Williams calls the 'wilderness' (in accordance with older translations of the Bible). It is there (so the text says) that she sees God face-to-face as a God who cares for her. This text describes an extraordinary theophany within biblical tradition, when God is seen face-to-face ('And she called the name of the Lord that spake unto her, Thou God seest me: for she said, Have I also here looked after him that seeth me?' Gen. 16. 13). The presence of God is defined as that of the one who cares for someone excluded by the dominant religion; as that of the one who cares for someone who arrives in a no-man's-land because she is 'different' from the 'others', and is no longer 'useful'. The God who 'cares' (the God of compassion) dwells in the borderland. The frontier areas are places where 'lovers' are to be found: those who break through borderland thinking and establish contact zones in the marginal areas, longing to achieve the impossible. New images appear there: of God as the one to look out for because he/she is always looking out for us beyond injustice and divisions; and of God as a beckoning horizon toward which we might possibly advance: the divine taking shape in clay vessels made from the shards of continually renewed and reconstructed economies of equality, and arising from subjugated knowledge with the power to fragment and scatter the dominant knowledge. The divine in this instance is a 'fragmented God', to invoke an image proposed by the French theologian Pohier.

Theologians in different contexts find themselves in pluralistic spaces where they are called on to be multilingual: to speak the language of religious understanding and that of science and scholarship, and to share the experience of living in new borderland spheres. Surprising things happen in these marginal areas that throw us off balance, as when one loses one's footing on a flight of stairs, misses the last step, and enters an indefinable space before it is possible to recover one's balance. There is a void between the moment of leaving the old environment and that of entry into a new reality.

New metaphors can be discovered one by one in the process, to be stored once again in earthenware vessels. Time after time, every day, fresh water, which is so scarce and valuable, has to be fetched, as by the woman on the tea plantation, in order to maintain a hazardous standard of life. The use of water and earth demands the skill and effort most readily afforded by the marginalized and by those who also have to live their lives on the edge, who are not afraid to soil their clothes and dirty their hands, and join the ranks of those who till the hard ground by the toil and sweat of their brow.

*Translated by J. Griffiths*

## Note

1. Pieris cites some brilliant examples in this respect. See: Aloysius Pieris, *Prophetic Humour in Buddhism and Christianity. Doing Interreligious Studies in the Reverential Mode*, Colombo, 2005.

## Literature

Aloysius Pieris, 'Interreligious Dialogue and Theology of Religions: An Asian Paradigm', *Horizons* 20/1 (1993), pp. 106-14

*Id.*, *Prophetic Humour in Buddhism and Christianity. Doing Interreligious Studies in the Reverential Mode*. Colombo, 2005.

Lynda Sexson, *Ordinarily Sacred*. New York, 1982.

Dolores Williams, *Sisters in the Wilderness. The Challenge of Womanist Godtalk*. New York, 1993.

# Religion as a Map of Salvation?
# Some Epistemological Changes

JOSÉ AMANDO ROBLES

If the impact of religious pluralism on the perception of religions can be of the order of a new paradigm, we should do well to take note of already current major changes of a more directly epistemological nature, as their impact will become even greater. When all is said and done, in a new framework of religious pluralism, religions will, even if their differences are relativized, still continue to see themselves as 'religions', as means and road maps leading to salvation as full human realization. But will they be that in the new framework? Will they be able to go on regarding themselves as such? Will they be able to go on reproducing themselves as 'religions', and shall we be able to go on calling them that?

It is questions such as these that underlie the present study, and this will deal with the following topics: some of the changes and/or elements that are shaping a new framework of knowledge; their incidence and impact on religions, especially on religions of salvation, as we have understood them; the crisis these are undergoing; religion in the new framework of understanding and of culture.

## I. Changes shaping a new framework of knowledge1

One of these changes is that reflected in our new way of perceiving time and even reality itself. Until a few decades ago, still within our cultural ambit, past, present, and future had a temporal density, were durations, in which the future was regarded as a prolongation of the present and knowledge was of capital importance in constructing this prolongation – a knowledge, whether inherited or 'discovered', of a reality that pre-existed us. Knowledge, like reality, also had density. Today that is no longer so. The present is pure construction, and the future and the past are resources for building that present – facts, outlook. Everything has become raw material, resource and instrument, including what we call reality and even knowledge itself.

This change is not without consequences for any form of knowledge, particularly for religions or religion. Now all knowledge has to show two things: that it is pertinent to the construction of the new present, and that it in turn is 'constructed', verified and verifiable – all this within the conditions of freedom and creativity that reality as construction requires. Received knowledge as such – revealed, believed, inherited or 'discovered' – is no longer registered. It has to demonstrate its pertinence and undergo specific verification.

In other words, knowledge has become praxic, and so has everything else with it. What is real is no longer what is physical, what exists as a fact of nature. What is real is what we construct, and reality exists insofar as it is constructed. And being praxic, knowledge has become determining. No longer because, as a matter of fact, it lies at the heart and origin of all human constructs, but because its systematic creation has now become a necessity for survival in the present. Systematic creation of knowledge, continuous application of this: as some writers declare, ours are societies that effectively live on change.

But if it is to be creative, knowledge has to be free. It cannot accept dogmas or beliefs, adherence to unverified truths or values. Only it, in its different forms and registers, can place limits on itself. Dogmas and beliefs would impede the necessary creation and self-correction. In fact, the new paradigm or matrix of knowledge does not have this sort of values attached to it. This is the first time this has happened in the history of humankind, and it has two major consequences: first, that religion will no longer be able to proceed as it has done in the past, articulating itself on the basis of the values that accompanied the past's paradigm of knowledge; second, that values, which we need more than ever in order to construct, direct, and guide the human project, will have to be formed by us, like everything else, in a process of trial and error.

Finally, in this context knowledge, in its different orders, is required to be specific, not redundant or duplicative. In the case of so-called religious knowledge, this too will have to be what it claims to be: specific, ultimate, and gratuitous, not philosophical, ethical, or anthropological. In this field duplication and redundancy become objects of suspicion, at best as unnecessary ballast, if not as inertia, and often as credal knowledge, unverified knowledge. On principle, of course, there is no limit to any sort of knowledge, nor can there be. But it will be required to be specific and to pass the test of its specificity.

## II. Impact of the new framework on religion

I began by saying that we need to take note of major changes already under way, on account of the equally major impact they may have on religions such as we have known them. Let us look at the facts.

The subjects for analysis and reflection still dominant in the theologies of the theist religions, and also in some theologies of religious pluralism, are 'objective' subjects or present themselves as such: God, salvation, sin, the universality and uniqueness of Christ in the case of Christianity, and so on. In the new framework 'objective' subjects have ceased to exist and, as a result, so has interest in them as 'objective' realities. It is as if religion had transmuted and in its transmutation had shed its former nature. There is still interest in these subjects, but in the measure that they are experience and can be experienced, not as 'objective' truths and, as such, beliefs. Objectivity with its pretensions to revelations and truths is collapsing.

Religion, in the new framework, is praxic. It is not something that pre-exists us: we have to construct it, and to construct it not anyhow, but experientially. It is an experience that has to be made. This is why Raymund Panikkar, in his considerations of Christianity, has been able to say that nothing would happen to the Christian faith even if all the scriptures were to disappear, provided that the *Eucharist* and *personal encounter* with Christ survived.[2] And the fact is that genuine religion as such is not scriptures or truths. Not is it a world-view, a value edifice, let alone a 'lifestyle'. If it were any of these, it would be very easy to be a Christian, just as it would be very easy to be a Muslim or a Buddhist. It would be a question of cultural identity and/or moral adherence. But it is much more than a matter of cultural iden-tification or moral adherence. It is a total involvement, the greatest work we can perform on ourselves, a new being, actually being the complete being that we are. What look like objective subjects in the religions of structures and systems are no more, in most cases, than expressions of what were successful, and therefore instructive, religious experiences. But they are not the experience in itself that others had, nor are they the one we are called to have. Its nature cannot be made into an object, nor are there scriptures that can contain it.

This praxic reality has to be specific, and this praxic reality that is specific, proper, that cannot be reduced to any other, is the ultimate creation human beings can attain – ultimate in the sense of quality, not of time. So ultimate that, although it is a human creation, it does not seem to be such when it comes about but is, on the contrary, experienced as a leap, as a grace, as something given. It appears to be beyond all effort, beyond all making. It is truly the ultimate. There is no other reality beyond it. It is the whole of reality.

In this sense religion in the West, which, although it has made so much use of art, particularly in its best cultural periods, has always seen itself more as a world-view and a philosophy than as an art, will now have to see itself more as the latter, because it shares with art being knowledge, experiential knowledge, creation, and the symbolic nature of its language.

And this is, in effect, the new being – which is also the oldest – that religion is discovering in the new framework of knowledge: being, like art, creation-knowledge and symbolic language. There is, however, one big difference: that where art ends – if it is possible to speak of art in this way – symbol and symbolism as creation, the religious experience, begin. Art, with all its sublimity, expresses itself in symbol and stops there. This is the essence of art: to remain expressed in the created work and, therefore, to be seen or heard in that, in artistic creations and not outside or beyond them. Religion also has to express itself symbolically and only symbolically. It cannot do so in any other manner. But in religion symbolism is not the terminus, it is barely the flight of an arrow aimed at experience. Because religious experience does not lie in the symbolic expression that has been given to it; it lies infinitely farther on, in experience itself. The symbol in art is destined to last, because otherwise art itself would perish. In religion, the symbol is a precursor and as a precursor is destined to perish.

Recuperating the symbolic nature of its language is a challenge facing religion in the new framework: this is a necessity. Otherwise, religion would descend into becoming a philosophy and an ethics, so redundant knowledge, not necessarily experiential on principle, still less specific and ultimate knowledge, while religion genuinely as such is ultimate – and only ultimate – experience.

As a result of this, religion cannot view itself as truth-bearing knowledge, but only as an experience of bottomless and formless gratuitousness and knowledge. Religion is not a world-view, nor is it a philosophy or an ethics. Its competence does not lie in the truths or Parmenidean concept that such systems suppose. If religion persists in being and presenting itself as a religion of truths, it automatically turns into a religion of beliefs. Because such truths will not be experience, let alone ultimate experience. Concepts and truths are tools on a far lower level than religious experience. They do not affect it. Religion's competence lies not in truths but in experience and the pointers to it: the best symbols being as indicative as they possibly can. We need truths and concepts to construct our world, but it falls to other human structures and faculties to supply them. Religion already has its own task, no small one but infinite, indeed, which it is discovering within the new framework of knowledge and from which its contributions can and must be literally infinite.

This task is, furthermore, deeply human, the most human there is, and, by the same token, lay, not religious. For it is not as though it were a task set apart, or a 'reality apart'. It is the one reality and the one human task, both of which have to be made, carried out, discovered, and lived in all their depth and all their fullness. This means that in a well-understood spirituality there is no possibility or escape or flight. Where could we escape from or fly to if there is no reality other than what there is in all its depth and radicalness? In this new perception it is religion that has to demonstrate that it is lay, human, deeply and totally human. This is why some authors speak of 'religion without religion'. Here too, in the end it is not the habit that makes the monk, not religious referents that make something religious, but the condition of what we call monk or religious: gratuitousness as experience, treasure, or pearl, and the undivided heart from which it emanates.

The impact of the new framework of knowledge on religion could not be greater: hence the need to 'rethink' religion.

## III. Crisis of the religion of truths and beliefs

Obviously, changes such as those indicated do not come about without causing a deep crisis in past religions. I am not going to expand on this here, since crisis in religion, even deep crisis, is now common parlance. I should, though, like to emphasize some important differences in how we evaluate and interpret this crisis.

The most sensible authors see the need to compare the present crisis with the religious changes that came about in the 'crux-epoch' or 'axial epoch', as Karl Jaspers called it, referring to the first millennium before Christ. They do not – and rightly – find more recent comparable events, which is a good indication of the historical significance of the crisis. But this is not enough, especially when the evaluation being made is predominantly cultural, as happens in most cases. It is not enough because, without taking account of the type of causes underlying the previous crisis, it cannot be evaluated properly, and these same limitations are carried through to evaluation and interpretation of the present crisis. An example of this is when some authors claim that there have been crises like this in the past and that Christianity has emerged unscathed from them; consequently, it will emerge unscathed from this one too. There are as yet no means of verifying this. We do know that, if we are to find a shift of equal significance to the present one, we need to go back to the Neolithic revolution, a revolution that originated phenomena such as that of the 'crux-epoch', the effects of which are still to be found even millennia later, and which, strictly speaking, has no parallel with any other revolution, is unheard-of. Suffice to note that no cultural paradigm in the past ceased to be mythic-symbolic; that is, none came into being without its corresponding values, with all that implies. For the first time in the history of the human race, the paradigm that makes our life possible is not axiological; the values we need, including religion, have to be created as we are creating everything else.

We need to go back to the Neolithic revolution because it was a society-work transformation that took place then, and this has been the basis of all later cultural transformations.[3] It was a profound structural transformation of way of life; that is, of the nature of the resources that underpin life, of the nature of the techniques employed to obtain these, and of the social organization needed to live in society on this material base. This is the same as would seem to have begun to happen in our time, and which we should lay down as a hypothesis. In the comparative dimensions affecting us today, cultural changes on their own explain very little.

Another limitation of the approach I am criticizing is that it finds it very difficult, if not impossible, to embrace the possibility that what is undergoing crisis is the paradigm itself, the religion of beliefs, together with its contents. And is that what is happening? There are many signs pointing in this direction. The crisis is not only that of Christianity but of all the religions in general insofar as they are religions of beliefs, and the crisis of Christianity is not simply that of the world-view it took over from Hellenism. It is all the 'received' paradigms that are in crisis, in all their categories and values. It is religions as systems of truths that no longer register; it is the religions of beliefs to which the religions of truths give rise that are in crisis, because their pretensions to objectivity and *logos* make the religious experience they proclaim and promise impossible, because they block it. The crisis is of a paradigm, of the agrarian paradigm, in which for several millennia religion successfully expressed itself, but which is no longer received, precisely to the degree that our societies are no longer agrarian or prepared to be seen as such. And the challenge is that of the gospel: new wine needs new bottles and new patches need new clothes, but this time it is expressed the other way round: new bottles and new clothes need new wine and new patches.

## IV. Religion in the new framework of knowledge and culture

New wine? Not so new, since Jesus of Nazareth was already talking of it two thousand years ago. In this sense, as regards the basic content, the new religion of which we speak is effectively old enough. What is new is that the new framework and context no longer leave any space for the old religion of truths and beliefs. This cannot reproduce itself from truths and beliefs; it can only reproduce itself from itself. And by reproducing itself from itself, it can only reproduce itself as bottomless and formless knowledge and experience.

There is no space for the old religion, and therefore neither is there space for the new and the old to coexist, as happened in the past. Furthermore, the new religion cannot make indiscriminate use of the language that characterized beliefs. If it does use it, it can only be by separating its signic or credential charge from its symbolic riches and never incorporating the former in the latter, since religious knowledge is a bottomless and formless knowledge.

The new religion will not, then, be able to reproduce itself as it did before, from truths and values, whether Greek or modern, since it is the character of truth or of value – its pretension to 'objectivity' – that causes the problem. Compared with that of the past, this is a truly new religion, which will therefore have to be called by another name. Unfortunately we have no such name and have to resign ourselves to using such unsatisfactory terms as spirituality, religious experience, interior life and way, or expressions such as religion without religion.

Nor will the new religion provide the map of the path or paths that lead to salvation, understanding this as the fullest realization human beings can achieve. Devalued as means to salvation, religions would like still to be seen as its representation, maps of the ways leading there. But this is not possible: they cannot play this role. Because, however paradoxical this may seem, they are not conceived or designed for this, to lead to full realization. They would provide very awkward maps, which whether one likes it or not would take the place of reality and lead only to themselves. Religions as we know them, religions of truths and therefore of beliefs, are in practice conceived and designed to make human beings believe in the existence of light and to behave in accordance with this faith, not to enable men and women to see or – better still – to be this light. Spiritual men and women from all religious traditions have been well aware of these limitations. Religions, like medieval stained-glass windows, only filter light; they do not lead to it, even if, by filtering it, they bear witness to its existence and in this sense enable people to know of it. But light has to reached by another route and in another manner, not through filters.

Without well-worn paths, the pluralism of ways, the genuine religious pluralism, is assured on principle, as are the lay, not religious, paths. More: it is the religious paths that will have to demonstrate that they are the right ones.

Finally, religion, in the new paradigm and context, in the new culture and type of society, has to be experience and total experience, of all one's being and from all the being we are – the greatest experience of which human beings are capable, a bottomless and formless experience; superior, by the same token, to any other; specific; irreducible; and therefore not even religious but uniquely and fully human.

*Translated by Paul Burns*

## Notes

1. For the bases and development of the argument made in this and succeeding sections see especially the works of Mariò Corbí: *Análisis epistemológico de las configuraciones axiológicas humanas*, Salamanca: Univ. de Salamanca, 1983; *Proyectar la sociedad, reconvertir la religión*, Barcelona: Herder, 1992; *Religión sin religión*, Madrid: PPC, 1996; *El camino interior. Más allá de las formas religiosas*, Barcelona: Bronce, 2001. See also J. Amando Robles, *Repensar la religión. De la creencia al conocimiento*, Heredia (Costa Rica): EUNA, 2001; the recent doctoral thesis by Teresa Guardans Cambó, *Indagaciones en torno a la condición fronteriza*, Barcleona: Univ. Pompeu Fabra, Oct. 2006; the publications of the annual Can Bordoi meetings in Barcelona, started in 2004 by CETR (Centre for the Study of Religious Traditions) to deepen and develop the subjects of religion and spirituality in knowledge societies (available at editorial.cetr.net); *Sociedades de conocimiento: Crisis de la religión y retos a al teología*, from the theological seminar held on 4–6 April 2005 at the National University, Heredia (Costa Rica); the journal *Alternativas*, 29 (Jan.–June 2005), Managua: Lascasiana, on the subject 'Crisis de la religión en Europa. ¿Nuevo lugar teológico?'

2. R. Panikkar, *Entre Dieu et le cosmos. Entretiens avec Gwendoline Jarczyk*, Paris, Albin Michel, 1998, p. 34. A few pages earlier, in similar vein, he wrote: 'The scriptures are useful to beliefs; they are superfluous to faith' (p. 29).

3. A thesis repeatedly postulated by Panikkar in a good number of his works, but perhaps never expressed with such pathos by anyone since Mircea Eliade, writing fifty years ago: 'As for the crisis of the modern world, we have to bear in mind that this world is ushering in an absolutely new type of civilization. It is impossible to foresee its future development. But it is useful to record that the only revolution that can be compared to it in the past of humankind, the discovery of agriculture, brought about spiritual upheaval and dismay on a scale we can only imagine.' (*Herreros y alquimistas*, Madrid: Alianza, 1974, p. 157).

# III. Practical Perspective

# The Transformation of Mission in the
# Pluralist Paradigm

PAUL F. KNITTER

In the life of individuals as well as of institutions, what at first sight looks like a danger often turns out to be an opportunity. I believe that this is the case when we try to relate the so-called pluralist paradigm for religious diversity with the mission of the Church. There are those in the Church who look upon the so-called pluralist theology of religions as a kind of Trojan horse, containing theologians who, once inside the walls of the Church, will destroy its missionary resources. A prominent example of such fear is Cardinal Ratzinger in *Dominus Iesus*. One can make the case that the dominant motivation for this declaration, as stated in its introduction and conclusion, is that 'The Church's constant missionary proclamation is endangered by relativistic theories' that lurk in the new pluralistic theologies of religions.[1]

In the following reflections I should like to suggest that such fears are based both on an understanding of the pluralist paradigm that incorrectly identifies this paradigm with relativism, and on an understanding of the church's mission that incorrectly identifies conversion as the primary purpose of mission. My thesis is that a correct understanding of the pluralist model will lead to a corrected, transformed, and revivified understanding of mission. What looks like a danger is really an opportunity.

## I. The pluralist paradigm: an affiirmation of both diversity and mutuality

Critics of pluralist theologians describe them as intent on affirming the plurality and the *equality* of religions. Herein lies one of the most prevalent

93

and unfortunate misunderstandings of the pluralist paradigm of religions. Pluralist theologians – at least those whom I associate with – seek to affirm the plurality and the *mutuality* of religions. In recognizing and affirming the diversity of traditions, pluralists are not interested in establishing the equality of all religions or the validity of the teachings of each religion. Rather, pluralists embrace and try to understand the diversity of religions in such a way as to promote the mutuality of religions, that is, the need and the possibility of relationships among the religious communities that will further the well-being of the religions and of the world. The primary intent of pluralist theology, you can say, is dialogue – to lay the foundations for a more effective and life-giving interaction among the religions.

This clarification of the pluralist model requires a kind of confession on the part of pluralist theologians. The motivational and the criteriological foundation or starting point for a pluralist theology of religions is the conviction that dialogue among the religious communities of the world is both necessary and possible. Such a conviction is rooted in their Christian faith, that is, in their understanding that Jesus' call to love our neighbours implies a call to dialogue with, respect, learn from, and cooperate with our neighbours, whatever religion they might belong to. But this conviction that dialogue is necessary and possible is also grounded in our common human experience of a world whose rampant violence and injustice can only be solved through a *dialogue of civilizations* rather than a *clash of civilizations*. 'Dialogue or Death,' the title of a book I contributed to a few decades ago, may be a bit sensational, but it is also disturbingly true.[2]

So the first item in the job description of a pluralist theologian is to explore and develop a theological understanding of religious diversity *and* of Christianity that will provide the groundwork for a more effective and honest inter-religious dialogue. Whatever pluralist theologians find in Christian teachings or practices that appears to be an obstacle to dialogue they approach with a 'hermeneutics of suspicion.' Whatever is opposed to dialogue is, at least implicitly, opposed to the gospel summons to love our neighbours and work with them for the Kingdom of God.

Pluralist theologians, therefore, are not out to relativize and assert the essential equality of all religions. They are aware of the profound, incorrigible diversity of religions. And they are aware, as well, that such diversity can lead not only to blissful harmony but also to uncomfortable discord. There is a need, in other words, to *assess* religious differences, or as one well-known pluralist has put it, 'to grade' different religious teachings and practices.[3] But in order to carry out this ranking in a dialogical, open-ended, non-violent way, pluralist theologians seek to provide what we may call *a level playing field* for the inter-religious dialogue. And they are convinced that such a level playing field is not possible if any one religion enters the field of dialogue believing and claiming that it has received from God or the Source of Truth the only or the full and final norm for all religious truth. How can the game of dialogue be fair if, before the game even starts, one team has been privileged and designated winner by the Referee?

In a pluralist theology, any claims of divinely-given religious superiority over all other religions are highly suspect. That doesn't mean that they are to be simply discarded; but they do require re-examination, re-interpretation, and re-possession.[4]

## II. Within the pluralist paradigm mission = dialogue

If we understand that the primary intent of the pluralist paradigm for religious diversity is to promote dialogue, and if we then explore the nature of dialogue, especially as the Roman Catholic Church has recently described it, we can draw the conclusion that the pluralist paradigm enables and challenges the Church to recognize that *mission is dialogue.*

Pope John Paul II's 1990 encyclical *Redemptoris Missio* (RM) and the declaration *Dialogue and Proclamation* (DP) issued jointly in 1991 by the Vatican Council for Inter-religious Dialogue and the Congregation for the Evangelization of Peoples, dropped what I would call revolutionary bombshells on traditional understandings of both mission and dialogue. Both announcements state that the Church's 'evangelizing mission' must include not only *proclamation* of the Good News of Jesus Christ (that's the traditional view of mission) but also, and just as much, *dialogue* with the good news in other religions (that's the bombshell!). Missionaries must not only proclaim and teach; they must also listen and learn![5]

But perhaps even more revolutionary is the understanding of dialogue in both RM and DP. In authentic dialogue, we are told, all sides have to be open to the following: (a) 'mutual enrichment' and 'advancement' – i.e. the possibility of learning something they didn't know;[6] (b) mutual 'questioning' and 'challenging' – i.e. the possibility of admitting mistakes;[7] and (c) the possibility of 'deciding . . . to leave one's previous spiritual or religious situation in order to direct oneself toward another'[8] – that is, in the dialogue one must be open to the possibility of changing sides! Here the Vatican is urging not only that Buddhists might become Christians but Christians, Buddhists! In these official statements, therefore, dialogue is understood as a relationship in which all sides are as committed to the necessity of speaking their minds as they are to the possibility of changing their minds.

Now, if, in obedience to the magisterium of the Church, this is the understanding of dialogue that Catholics should adopt as they seek to carry out the mission of the Church, then pluralist theologians would point out that there really is no difference between 'mission' and 'dialogue'. Pope John Paul II and the Vatican Congregations tell us that mission must include both proclaiming Christian truth and opening oneself to the possible truth in other religions. But that's the definition of dialogue – to speak and listen, to witness and be witnessed to. Dialogue, by its very nature, includes proclamation. To try to separate proclamation from dialogue would be like trying to separate hydrogen from water: you'd have hydrogen but you wouldn't have water. As water requires both hydrogen and oxygen, dialogue requires both proclamation and openness – speaking one's own truth and listening to that of others. Mission, defined as speaking and listening, is dialogue.

But if it is, then whatever obstructs dialogue, obstructs mission. In the pluralist paradigm, therefore, authentic missionary work can no longer be carried out for the purpose of establishing the superiority of Christianity over all other religions or to 'fulfill' or 'include' all other religious traditions in the full and definitive truth of the Christian Church. To base mission-as-dialogue on the conviction that God has given Christians the 'fullness of truth' and the exclusive and definitive norm for all truth does indeed allow the Christian missionaries to proclaim their truth; but it does not allow them really to listen to the truth of others to the extent that they are ready, as the Vatican says they should be, to be challenged, corrected, and to learn more. To what is 'full' one cannot add 'more'. To what is 'final' no changes can be made. To ground the motivation and purpose of mission on claims of Christian superiority over all religions is to obstruct authentic dialogue. And that would mean to undermine the true mission of the Church.

But if the ultimate purpose of missionary work, according to the pluralist paradigm, is no longer to establish the Christian Church as the superior and final revelation and religion over all others, then what is it?

## III. Purpose of mission *ad extra* and *ad intra*

From a pluralist perspective the purpose of missionary activity is twofold; it includes what missionaries seek to achieve both '*ad extra*', for the world, and '*ad intra*', for the inner life of the Church. The latter is a means to the former.

*Ad extra*: Pluralist theologians of religions would agree with what I believe is the general viewpoint of mainline Christian, especially Catholic, missiologists: the purpose, the *ratio sufficiens*, of mission, as of the entire life and activity of the Church, is *regnocentric* rather than ecclesiocentric.[9] Certainly, missionary work seeks, as I learned in the 1950s and 1960s, the *'plantatio ecclesiae'*. But planting the Church is not the primary end or goal of mission; indeed, it is a means to the primary end. The end that provides the focus and the norm for all missionary work is the same end that was the focus and norm of Jesus' mission and ministry: the *Basileia tou Theou.*

Scripture scholars and seekers after 'the historical Jesus' don't agree on much. But on this they do: that the core content and intent of Jesus' Good News was God's *Basileia*, which might best be translated into contemporary, non-patriarchal English as *the Commonwealth of God*.[10] Jesus' primary purpose, that which guided his ministry, was not to establish a Church; it was not to make sure that all people would recognize him as the only Saviour and Son of God; it was not even to bring people to a faith in God as the source of all being. Faith in God by itself was not enough.[11] It had to be the kind of faith in the kind of God that would inspire and strengthen people to believe in and work for, to the point of death, the Commonwealth of God.

Perhaps one of the most concise descriptions of what this Commonwealth of God meant for Jesus can be found in the simple sentence of Irenaeus: *'Gloria Dei vivens homo'*. And today we might add, *'vivens terra'*. The glory and the commonwealth of God are found in the continued life and well being of humanity and the earth. John B. Cobb, Jr., offers a description of the Commonwealth of God that is closer to the Synoptics: it was characterized by the healing of the sick, the release of prisoners, and freeing people from guilt. The thirsty receive water, the hungry are fed, the naked are clothed. To come into the fellowship that foreshadows the Commonwealth of God, the rich must share their wealth. Within that fellowship, the boundaries that separate people are erased. Sinners – that is, people who do not fulfill the law – eat with those who do. Loving relations supersede obedience to the law as the character of the Commonwealth.[12]

This, then, is the primary goal of Christian mission-as-dialogue: to engage other religions, and anyone who is interested, in the kind of dialogue that will promote what Christians symbolize as the *Basileia* or Commonwealth of God. This Commonwealth, as Jesus proclaimed it, was essentially eschatological: both already and not yet, here but still more to come. Therefore, it remains unfinished, not fully known, and so it can be worked toward only through a dialogical and cooperative effort of many perspectives. This, again, describes missionary endeavour: to witness to what we know of the *Basileia* through Jesus, but also to receive the witness of how other traditions and spiritualities seek to promote the well-being of humans and the earth.

At this point, postmodern critics might accuse Christian missionaries and pluralist theologians of 'promoting their own agenda' when they hold up the Commonwealth of God as the primary concern of their dialogue with others. To such an accusation, I can respond as a missionary and pluralist: 'Happily guilty!' This is indeed the agenda Christians bring to the dialogue; perhaps it is their distinctive contribution. Or expressed more cautiously, this is the *common ground* that Christians propose for the inter-religious dialogue. But it is proposed *dialogically*. That means: it recognizes that other religions may have other agendas and other proposals for common starting points for the dialogue. There need not be one and only common ground! There can be different starting points and agendas in different contexts and times. None of these common grounds must necessarily exclude the others; indeed, they must all try to include each other. Christian missionary-dialoguers will expect that if the agendas or primary concerns of other faith traditions are indeed true and of God, if they yield ethical fruits of peace and compassion, they will be further ways of fostering the well-being that constitutes the Commonwealth of God.

But where, some Christian critics will ask, does this leave the issue of conversions? Does mission-as-dialogue leave any room for the seeking of converts? It certainly does. Dialogue, as I said, consists of both the 'hydrogen and oxygen' of proclaiming and listening. And when one proclaims one's religious convictions, one is not satisfied with just sharing information. Rather, one wants the information to seep into, convince, and enlighten the mind and heart of one's dialogue partner. One wants one's partner to see and feel and be moved by the truth that animates one's own life. In a broad but also deep sense, this is conversion.

The truth that one witnesses to is meant to bring change into the life of the dialogue partner; the change will not necessarily, or not normally, bring about a change of the other's religious community. But it will deepen, clarify, modify, maybe even transform that religious identity. The Buddhist or Muslim, having heard and been converted to Jesus' message about the Commonwealth of God, will become a 'better' Buddhist or Muslim – just as the Christian, having heard Buddha's insistence on meditation or Islam's affirmation of the necessary link between faith and politics, might become a better Christian.

But it can happen that the witness of Jesus' Good News given in dialogue can lead to the kind of conversion that moves a person, as DP puts it, 'to leave one's previous spiritual or religious situation in order to direct oneself toward another.'[13] The Buddhist may decide to join the Christian community (or the Christian may decide to join the Buddhist *sangha*). Such conversions are not sought after. But if they occur, and as long as they occur freely and with integrity, they are welcomed. They are the result of human freedom, particular personal needs, and the unseen movements of the Spirit.

*Ad intra*: Such conversions from one religious community to another are an aspect – only one aspect – of the second goal of mission-as-dialogue. This goal has certain similarities to what in the past has been called the *planting* of the Church into new cultures. But it is much more accurately and engagingly described as the *liberation* of the Church from one culture in order to be *incarnated* into another.

Since the Second Vatican Council, there has been much talk among ecclesiologists and missiologists of what Karl Rahner called 'the World Church'. Rahner believed that the Vatican II Fathers, after some 1500 years of church history, had reopened magisterial doors and enabled the Church to evolve from the Roman Catholic Church into the truly Catholic Church (though, Rahner added, had the bishops clearly realized what they were doing, they might have held back!).[14] In affirming the value of other religions and cultures, in recognizing that the Church has something to learn from these others, in calling for liturgical and doctrinal expression in and through these religious cultures, the Fathers of Vatican II were calling for not just the *implanting* of the Church in new cultural soil; they were encouraging the growth of new species of church life in new cultural and religious environments. They were unlocking the doors to what has been called the 'Latin [or European] Captivity of the Church[15] and allowing the freed prisoners to become truly an African or an Asian or a Latin American Church. This is not an implantation of the old; it is the incarnation of something new.

And this liberation, this incarnation of 'new species' of the one Church, will take place mainly through the Church's mission-as-dialogue. Through a genuinely dialogical engagement with other religions and cultures, missionaries – especially those who have grown up in these cultures – will enable the Church to learn and so to develop into 'new ways of being Church'.[16] Missionaries, we might say, are midwives who tend the birth of Rahner's vision of a truly World Church.

So I would humbly suggest to Cardinal Ratzinger, now Benedict XVI, that his fears are exaggerated. The pluralist paradigm of mission-as-dialogue is not the destruction but the transformation of the Church's mission; it is an opportunity rather than danger. It can inspire future generations of missioners who will nurture a World Church that, with other religions, will more effectively build the Commonwealth of God.

## Notes

1. See sections 4 and 23. See also Paul F. Knitter, 'The Abiding Task of the Church to Proclaim the Uniqueness of Jesus' in Thomas Malipurathu and L. Stanislaus (eds.), *The Church in Mission: Universal Mandate and Local Concerns*, Gujarat Sahitya Prakash: Anand, 2002, pp. 117–19 (116–46).
2. John B. Cobb, Jr., Monika Hellwig, Leonard Swidler, and Paul F. Knitter, *Death or Dialogue: From the Age of Monologue to the Age of Dialogue*, Philadelphia: Trinity International, 1990.
3. John Hick, 'On Grading Religions', *Religious Studies* 17 (1981), pp. 451–67.
4. Just how this can be done is, of course, not the topic for this essay. Examples of attempts to develop an orthodox Christian theology of religions that moves beyond models of 'inclusivism' or 'fulfillment' are Alan Race, *Interfaith Encounter: The Twin Tracks of Theology and Dialogue*, London: SCM Press, 2001; John Hick, *The Rainbow of Faiths: Critical Dialogue on Religious Pluralism*, London: SCM Press, 1995; Paul F. Knitter, *Jesus and the Other Names: Christian Mission and Global Responsibility*, Maryknoll, NY: Orbis, 1996; Michael Amaladoss, *Making Harmony: Living in a Pluralist World*, Delhi: ISPCK, 2003; Marjorie Hewitt Suchocki, *Divinity and Diversity: A Christian Affirmation of Religious Pluralism*, Nashville: Abingdon Press, 2003; Reinhold Bernhardt, *Ende des Dialogs? Die Begegnung der Religionen und ihre theologische Reflexion*, Zürich: Theologischer Verlag, 2005; Jeannine Hill Fletcher, *Monopoly on Salvation? A Feminist Approach to Religious Pluralism*, New York: Continuum, 2005; Perry Schmidt-Leukel, *Gott ohne Grenzen: Eine christliche und pluralistiche Theologie der Religionen*, Gütersloh: Gütersloher Verlaghaus, 2005; José María Vigil, *Teología del Pluralismo Religioso: Curso sistemático de teología popular*, Quito: Abya Yala, 2005.
5. This revolutionary understanding of dialogue as an essential part of mission was already suggested in 1984 when the Vatican Secretariat for Non-Christian Religions issued *The Attitude of the Church toward the Followers of Other Religions*. See especially sections 13 and 29
6. RM 55,56
7. DP 32; RM 56
8. DP 41
9. Stephen B. Bevans and Roger P. Schroeder, *Constants in Context: A Theology of Mission for Today*, Maryknoll, NY: Orbis, 2004, chs 10 and 12.
10. See John B. Cobb, Jr., 'Commonwealth and Empire', in David Ray Griffin,

John B. Cobb, Jr., Richard A. Falk, and Catherine Keller, *The American Empire and the Commonwealth of God: A Political, Economic, Religious Statement*, Louisville: Westminster/John Knox Press, 2006, pp. 137–50.

11. Jon Sobrino, *Spirituality of Liberation: Toward a Political Holiness*, Maryknoll, NY: Orbis, 1988, pp. 83–4.

12. Cobb, ibid., p. 145.

13. See Note 8.

14. Karl Rahner, 'Toward a Fundamental Theological Interpretation of Vatican II', *Theological Studies* 40 (1979), pp. 716–27.

15. John Robinson, *Truth Is Two-Eyed*, Philadelphia: Westminster, 1980, p. x.

16. See Thomas C. Fox, *Pentecost in Asia: A New Way of Being Church*, Maryknoll, NY: Orbis, 2002.

# Rethinking Pluralism:
# from Inculturation to 'Inreligionation'

ANDRÉS TORRES QUEIRUGA

The problems posed by pluralism and the encounter with, and influence of, other religions have always existed. But the fact that we now have to face them with a previously unsuspected intensity shows that they have entered a new phase. In Christianity – from which the present study takes its focus, while opening out to others – the break with the past marked by the modern age has imposed both an intense *internal* critique and a serious approach to the *real* encounter with other religions. But both the magnitude of the change and institutional resistance have resulted in partial solutions and *ad hoc* resources, as challenges appeared, rather than radical re-interpretation. Consequently, responses have multiplied profusely; they therefore appear notably asynchronous in their internal resources: properly updated ideas can appear alongside largely outdated ones. Or old ideas, once updated, can even continue effectively influencing the previous presumptions.

## I. The new presumptions: the idea of revelation

Pluralism affects no less than our central concept, that of *revelation*. The traditional view of this was absolutely solid in conceiving of revelation as a divine oracle or *diktat*, miraculous in character. And this necessarily implied the idea of 'choosing' (a mediator and his people), turning revelation into an 'exclusive' privilege. Over against *divine* revelation and inspiration to the *chosen* people stood *human* religious endeavour (if not 'the work of the devil'); over against *supernatural* religion stood the *natural* religions. Outside the Bible there 'could not' be revelation, just as outside the Church there could be no salvation.

Fortunately, this conception has been superseded.[1] When the Enlightenment submitted the sacred texts to criticism – described by Schweitzer as 'the most powerful (*das Gewaltigste*)' and daring thing ever undertaken by religious awareness – it forced us to understand the inevitable human mediation of revelation. Once it was no longer identified with the letter of the Bible, it became possible to see revelation in other religions as well: once literalism goes, exclusivism has to follow. But assimilating all this requires a real revolution, and we have still not drawn all the consequences. Until Vatican II it had not entered – and then, how cautiously! – into official theology. Even today its presence is very timid and has not really changed mental attitudes. This makes some pointers important.

It is not enough to affirm the intrinsic nature of revelation; we have to go to its deepest root: *creation through love*. As *creatio continua*, this is a sustaining and onward-moving presence: it did not create us *in illo tempore*, deistically abandoning us on earth while itself staying in heaven. Not being moved by need or lack, God creates only *out of love*: God creates men and women to be sons and daughters not 'for his own glory and service' but so that they can reach the greatest fulfilment possible. This is why God's greatest concern is to show himself to them and save them. Does a decent father or mother who would not try as much for his or her children exist? A human mother might forget, but God will never forget (Isa. 49.15). And, since God's is 'a greater love than can be conceived',[2] if there are limitations in this process, these cannot derive either from God's reserve – or, contrary to certain fashions, from his 'silence'! – or from his meanness.

Revelation thus loses its character of an isolated, miraculous, or arbitrary process. There is no longer a God who would 'dictate' his truths to a select few, leaving the rest abandoned; who 'would reveal' late and obscurely what he could have revealed earlier and clearly. What we have instead is rather God's ceaseless 'loving struggle' to make himself known, overcoming the darkness and resistance of creatures. And on the human side, what we have is a sort of 'catching on' to that God who is speaking to us in reality, in history, and in life. Let us be clear on this: we catch on because we discover the *reality* of God's presence;[3] not because God wants to hide and we surprise him, as in a children's game of hide-and-seek, but because God wants to show himself to us: 'Surely the Lord is in this place – and I did not know it!' (Gen. 28.16).

This means that there has *never* been *anyone*, man or woman, individual, society, or culture, born unprotected from God's unconditional love and to whom or which God does want to show himself to the greatest extent possible. This is the purpose of religions, which exist precisely to harness and welcome – more or less completely – this Presence. This is why they all see themselves as revealed. And they all are, in the strict sense: resistance to accepting this – still partially present in Vatican II, which spoke only of religious *values* and not of *revelation* in other religions[4] – is explained by the habit of continuing to speak of *the* revelation, since we then, by tautological imposition, think only of *the* biblical revelation. But we have only to put this in the plural, speaking of *revelations*,[5] to understand that they happen in *all* religions, insofar as what makes them is human acceptance of the real and revealing divine presence. From the standpoint of faith, we have only to think of atheist denial to draw the true consequence: *all religions are true*. Not because *everything* in them, including the biblical one, is true, but to the extent – but *real* extent – to which they welcome the Presence.

## II. Asymmetric pluralism

The conclusion is so decisive that it would merit a detailed analysis. Here there is space to indicate just two basic consequences, which Roger Haight expresses thus: the first, directly theological, is that since no one has ever lacked creating-saving love, we have to accept a true religious *pluralism*, because 'the revelation of God present in the religions possesses a historical autonomy that enters into a dialectical relationship with Christianity and the other religions, and not into a dependency.' The second, simply realistic historically, is that 'this does not mean that all religions are equally revelatory'.[6] This second conclusion stems from the fact that, while God's love is universally unrestricted, *human* reception of it inevitably turns out to be unequal, both within the history of each religion, which means there is progress, and between the various religions, where *subjective* respect cannot mask undeniable *objective* differences and 'degrees'.[7] Choosing one religion should not be a matter of irresponsible caprice.

This is why, while accepting a pluralist basis as necessary, I prefer to speak of *asymmetric pluralism*. This is an imperfect category, as are all on this still shifting scene, but it does (a) allow the conjuncture of realism and respect and (b) postulate the need for dialogue. *Respect*, because, without denying the fact of differences, it unequivocally recognizes true revelation in all religions; *dialogue*, because within the 'horizontal' asymmetry among religions, it recognizes the more fundamental 'vertical' relationship of them all to God. No religious configuration can exhaust the infinite riches of the *Deus semper maior* who, overflowing any special understanding, edges everyone toward the common mystery. Welcoming this mystery means taking advantage of all lights, offering one's own and welcoming those of others. The riches of the other do not impoverish but enrich. Dialogue constitutes true faithfulness and is a criterion of sincere search. Anything else would be pride or 'demoniacal' hoarding.[8]

From this perspective I think it also fair to speak of a *Jesuanic theocentrism*, which, recognizing God as the absolute centre, as Jesus did, confesses Jesus as the one who opened *in history* the decisive and incomparable keys to the mystery of God. I stress 'in history' because, without having recourse to concepts like the 'cosmic Christ', it allows us to speak of insuperable culmination in what Jesus revealed (this possibility also appears in cultural discoveries, such as the illegitimacy of slavery). Besides, by speaking of culmination, it *implies* recognizing what other prophets or founders have discovered as revealed. By the same token, it also implies a summons to welcome this, since any realization in history is necessarily imperfect and perfectionable: Christianity should learn from other religions anything that might complete understanding and fulfilment of what is revealed in Jesus. And, finally, it implies recognizing the right of all *on principle* to speak of their own 'theo- or mysterio-centrism', since choosing cannot mean decreeing *a priori* one's own truth or another's exclusion from truth, but has to be an *a posteriori* preference, once the various reasons for it have been examined and discussed.

## III. From 'inculturation' to 'inreligionation'

The above observations, cruelly summary, were needed to clarify my principal proposition: the need to complete 'inculturation' with 'inreligionation'. To complete, not to supplant, since I believe inculturation represents a great advance and an undeniable requirement.

The culturally mediated nature of revelation means that it never exists 'in a pure state' but is always interpreted from a historical context, within determined cultural categories. There is no religion that is not inculturated. Every change supposes a cultural re-modelling. This came about originally in a quite fundamental way with the entry of the biblical tradition into the Greek and Roman world, and it happened again with each advance made by Christianity: 'A faith that does not become culture is a faith that has not been fully received, nor wholly considered, nor wholly experienced' (Pope John Paul II, 1982).

*Inculturation*, in making this plain, undoubtedly marked an enormous theoretical step forward, with very important consequences for real encounter among religions. It is easy to understand the wide acceptance of this 'fine neologism',[9] not only by theologians but also by the official magisterium: 'Through inculturation the Church makes the Gospel incarnate in different cultures and at the same time introduces peoples, together with their cultures, into her own community. She transmits to them her own values, at the same time taking good elements that already exist in them and renewing them from within.'[10]

Despite this, it has met with major objections. The main ones are (a) that it can lead to imperialism by one culture – generally western – over the others[11] and (b) that it 'presupposes the idea of a universal theology [. . .] pre-existent of itself in a non-inculturated version'.[12] It is worth summarizing its danger, showing that the semantic power of the word can suggest that the encounter should respect culture but may suppress (or ignore) religion. This danger was real and still has great validity in the collective consciousness.[13] History provides a terrible warning on this: persecution of faithful and priests, burning of sacred texts, destruction of places of worship, efforts at erasing religious imagery, and repeated attempts to demolish traditions.

But to let the possibility of abuse entail the suppression of use would produce an irreparable loss. The proper course would be to keep inculturation whilst correcting and completing it. Doing so is possible and even obligatory, given the new perception.

## IV. Inreligionation

Once we recognize real revelation in every religion, it becomes clear that there can be no case for suppressing it: this would mean suppressing or denying a real presence of God. The encounter can be legitimated only in order to give and/or receive an improvement: offering what we judge to be helpful to the other and receiving what might help us from the other. For example, what a Christian missionary could *offer* might be: an important aspect lacking (the personal nature of God), a correction (the wrongness of human sacrifice), or an undiscovered depth (God as pure love and unconditional forgiveness). What the missionary might *receive* in return could be: the greatest concern to keep divine oneness and sovereignty (from Islam), 'non-activist' reception of grace (from Hinduism), or the ineffability of the divine Mystery (from Buddhism).

It is evidently always the other who should understand, judge, and where proper accept what is being offered. 'Inculturation' shows that this cannot happen by denying one's own *culture*, but within and from it. So, then, something strictly parallel happens with religion: the one who listens is a religious person who, on the basis of his/her own religion, accepts and discriminates (or denies) what is being put forward. This what 'inreligionation' seeks to suggest; it may be an ugly word, but its heart is generous and fraternal. It clarifies and foments a genuine attitude of both welcome and offering.

*Welcome*: those who truly live with God cannot simply renege on the tradition that nourished and moulded their religious experience. This inevitably forms the basis and framework for their understanding and distinguishing, for acceptance or rejection. Welcoming will then mean not simply abandoning one's own religion but accepting an addition or even a correction *from within* it. God always remains the same: it is our understanding and experience that improve. It is not, then, a matter of razing our own religion, leaving 'culture' free to implant a new religious offer *ex novo*. Rather, while keeping our own religious-cultural unity intact, we have to use it as a base from which to assimilate – 'inculturate and inreligionate' – whatever may improve it.

*Offering*: proclaiming God cannot be done against God, but always trying to improve the grasp, expression, and consequences of God's presence in life. There has been too much abuse by the intolerant totalitarianism of all or nothing: if my religion is true, then yours is false; if you accept mine, you have to destroy yours.[14] Since it is *the same God* that is present in all religions, the attitude should be: my religion is true, but so is yours; since God is always greater than our understanding, we should complement one another. The best of my tradition belongs to you as much as to me; this is why I offer it to you, if it convinces you; and I also welcome the best of yours, because I feel it to be just as much mine. Putting aside excluding and intolerant routines, we should once more learn the great truth of love: everything is for everyone, since the same and only God seeks to be for all.

Unfortunately, the clarity of the principle has to take account of the difficulty in practice and the reality of differences: dialogue with the great religions cannot be the same thing as dialogue among certain ethnic or tribal religions. But the spirit of respect, dialogue, offering, and welcome can and should hold sway at all meetings.

## V. The (implicit) presence of 'inreligionation'

The *word* is new and certainly seems somewhat strange. Personally, apart from its wide acceptance among liberations theologians,[15] I have found only two explicit mentions of it, by Alonso Pieris[16] and K. P. Aleaz,[17] who use 'enreligionization' and 'enreligionazation'.

Whatever its form, its *content* has a universal presence. It begins with St Paul, who describes the relationship of Christianity to Judaism as 'grafting in' (see Rom. 11.16–24): in grafting, the receptor tree is not suppressed but enriched with a new element, which in its turn receives living-space and sap that it did not have before. One could multiply quotations that imply the same,[18] and there is no doubt that it is implied in the various terms coined to overcome the excessive exclusivism-inclusivism dichotomy, such as 'pluralist inclusivism', 'mutual inclusivism', 'inclusivist reciprocity', 'mutual benefit', and so on.

In actual fact, inreligionation has happened and continues to happen. It is present, most intensely, in the sacred books themselves: How many concepts, prayers, psalms, and institutions came from outside the Bible: from Mari, from Egypt, from Babylon . . .? Was not prophetism itself an importation in the first place? And so it goes on: How much has Islam not received from the other 'religions of the book', and how much has it influenced Christianity and Judaism? Can present-day Judaism and Christianity be thought of – and the same is true for Hinduism and Buddhism – without their powerful mutual influence? Are there missionaries whose faith has not been influenced by those they are influencing?

Furthermore, at the summits of religious experience, among mystics, religious communion in depth tends even to erase cultural differences. This produces the significant *practical phenomenon*, which has deep spiritual and theological implications, of persons who, deeply immersed in two religious traditions, experience both as their own. This double religious adherence is (still) exceptional, but it may well multiply, which will give us a lot to think about and perhaps to do in the future. Current cases are those who, like Raymund Panikkar and Henri Le Saux, regard themselves as Hindu-Christians. Such cases do, of course, raise questions deserving of careful consideration,[19] but this does not deny their significance.

Perhaps even more significant is the existence of a *real ecumenism*, which is cross-fertilizing the various confessions, sometimes without even any warning. This is very clear among Christian confessions, through their greater affinity with one another and the greater degree of contact among them. But history today is increasingly rapidly bringing all the religions closer; influences of one on the others are multiplying, bringing about a transformation that is as silent as it is fruitful. This phenomenon is evident between the religions of the East and Christianity. Political conflicts are making calm cross-currents with Islam more problematic for the time being, but contact and time are clearly working in favour of future progress. With regard to ethnic religions, 'inreligionation' – experienced in the missions and developed in theological studies – is continually more obvious and fruit-ful, in Africa, Asia, and America.

Of course we must still be realists. But this should not exclude hope, let alone working toward the goal. It is no small achievement for the mentality of rivalry and exclusive suppression to be giving way to an attitude of respectful acceptance and fraternal collaboration. In my view, while accept-ing the need to adjust formal classifications of exclusiveness, inclusiveness, and pluralism as far as possible, we should stress more basic and compre-hensive categories. Having accepted the need for 'inculturation' is a great help. 'Inreligionation', by removing some misunderstandings, can make the process even more fruitful. In any case, we are now in the position where we can appreciate the huge importance of this real ecumenism – *in actu exercito* – represented by the continuous and growing mutual influence of all the religions: a strictly *religious* influence.

*Translated by Paul Burns*

## Notes

1. Rahner, Schillebeeckx, and Pannenberg are especially significant names, with a wide following: see, *e.g.*, D. Tracy, *The Analogical Imagination*, New York: Crossroad, 1981; H. Verweyen, *Gottes leztes Wort*, Regensburg: Pustet, ⁵2002; J. Werbick, *Der Glauben verantworten*, Freiburg: Herder, 2000; C. Theobald, *La révélation*, Paris: Atelier, 2001. See also my *La revelación de Dios en la realización del hombre*, Madrid: Cristiandad, 1987 (soon to appear in an updated edition).

2. This is how Bonaventure translated the great principle of Anselm: '[Vide igitur et attende, quoniam optimum quod simpliciter est] quo nihil melius cogitari potest' (*Itin. mentis in Deum* VI, 2).

3. Not 'as a mere subjective perception', as the Pastoral Instruction on theology and secularization in Spain (30 Mar. 2000) interprets it. I make some comments in 'Revelación como "caer na conta": razón teolóxica e maxisterio pastoral', *Encrucillada* 149/30 (2006), pp. 357–73.

4. 'Elements of truth and grace'; 'all that is good'; 'the riches'; 'as much as is true and holy'; 'glimmer of the truth that enlightens all human beings'; 'spiritual, moral and socio-cultural values'. . . See the detailed analysis by J. Castanyé, *Diàleg interreligiós i Cristianisme*, Barcelona, 2005, pp. 25–69.

5. See the article by Paulo Suess in this issue. For what follows, to soften the impression of dogmatism that might arise from a very compressed presentation, I refer to my *Diálogo de las religiones y autoconciencia cristiana*, Santander: Estella, 2005.

6. 'Pluralist Christology as Orthodoxy', in P. F. Knitter (ed.). *The Myth of Religious Superiority*, Maryknoll, NY: Orbis, 2005, p. 157. This coincidence with Haight shares the same foundations: saving creation. I had found the same concordance with regard to resurrection: just as Haight indicates in his *Jesus, Symbol of God* (Orbis, 1999, p. 147), my *Repensar la resurrección* (Madrid, 2003, pp. 213–4), tries to establish that Jesus' resurrection is not the first in time but a definitive revelation of principle: God is raising all to life and always has been.

7. I allude to John Hick, 'On Grading Religions', *Religious Studies* 17 (1981), pp. 451–67. Without going into discussion here, the allusion is illustrative: see my book, cited above. In any case, there is validity in Knitter's call to seek 'criteria that have an innate inner protection against the possibility that they might turn into arguments for exploitation, and which can obtain general assent in the world of academics and in the field of inter-religious encounter' ('Un diálogo necesario: entre la teología de la liberación y la teología del pluralismo', in J. M. Vigil, ed., *Por los muchos caminos de Dios* I, Quito: Abya Yala. 2003. p. 107).

8. Christoph Schwöbel, *Christliche Glaube im Pluralismus*, Tübingen: Mohr Siebeck, 2003, pp. 148–52.

9. *Catechesi tradendae*, n. 53.

10. *Redemptoris missio*, n. 52.

11. R. F. Betancourt, *Sobre el concepto de interculturalidad*, Mexico City, 2004.

12. Aloysius Pieris, 'The Problem of Universality and Inculturation with Regard to Patterns of Theological Thinking', *Concilium* 1994/6, pp. 70–69.

13. Joseph Ratzinger, who on occasions stresses cultural-religious solidarity, states that 'the Christian proclamation linked with philosophy, not with religions' (*Fe, verdad y tolerancia*, Salamanca, 2005, p. 171).

14. In the biblical tradition, furthermore, this was reinforced by the *henotheist schema*, which antedates monotheism (strict only after the Exile): *my god* is for me; others have theirs. Therefore I should protect my god *against* them, denying theirs and if necessary fighting and exterminating them. Let us consider that this was probably the original sense of 'You shall love the Lord your God with all your heart . . .' (Deut. 6.5). These schemas, once engraved on our minds, are not easily erased: we should, for example, take far more care over how we *pray* the Psalms.

15. Especially A. Soares and J. M. Vigil: it also appears in the excellent series 'Por los muchos caminos de Dios' ['Down God's many paths'], vols. I–IV, 2003–6, produced by the Association of Third World Theologians.

16. I found the reference in *Liberation, Inculturation, and Religious Dialogue*, p. 117, where it refers to *An Asian Theolgy of Liberation* (Maryknoll, NY: Orbis, 1988), p. 52. From Japan his Spanish translator Hoan Ribera pointed me to its initial appearance in 'Western Models of Inculturation: How far are they applicable in non-Semitic Asia?' in *East Asia Pastoral Review*,1985/2, pp. 116–24.

17. 'Pluralism calls for Pluralistic Inclusivism', in *The Myth of Religious Superiority*, *op.cit.*. p. 172. No one includes the word in the Index!
18. *E.g.* M. Amaladoss: 'Changing from a popular religious tradition to a major religion does not mean abandoning the first for the second but, in one way or another, trying to ingrate the one with the other' (*El evangelio en el encuentro de las culturas*, Bilbao, 1988, p.41).
19. 'Shall we have to come to say without paradox that there is a Christian manner of being a Hindu, a Buddhist, a Confucian?': C. Geffré, cited by G. Comeau, *Grâce à l'autre*, Paris, 2004, pp. 147–8. 'We need to ask if it is possible, and up to what point, to co-divide two different religious faiths, making both one's own and living both at the same time in one's own religious life' (J. Dupuis, *Jesus Christ at the Encounter of World Religions*, Maryknoll, NY: Orbis, 1991).

# Christianity and Religious Cosmopolitanism: Toward Reverse Universality

FELIX WILFRED

Defining the human cannot be the prerogative of any one single civilization, as much as envisioning the future destiny of humanity and its unity can be the privilege of any one religion. Never before has the future of humanity been so critical and elusive as it is today, calling for mobilization of resources from every quarter for its common construction. Never before in history has human co-existence been so vigorously debated as it is today – something that has resulted from the innumerable forms of human encounter the present-day life has thrown up. In the face of the sea of challenges confronting the entire human family, the claims of religions to their exclusive identities could be as much real and serious as children's playful construction of castles and fortresses on the sands of the shore. While divisions are deepening day by day with escalation of war and mass-murder, starvation and new forms of exclusion, the single most urgent question is about the *destiny of the human family and its salvation.*

It is this vision of the future of the whole of human family that should take hold of Christianity today, and it should be the key-conception to define its (Christianity's) relationship with other religious traditions. For too long, questions of Christology, soteriology, and ecclesiology have made up the nodal points for determining this relationship, turning Christianity in the process into a *'religio incurvata in se'* (a religion bent on itself). Much time and energy have been expended in disentangling the knot Christianity created for itself, leading to the proliferation of theologies of religion – grist to the academic mill. The challenge is to allow the thread of conversation with other religious traditions to stretch to the vast future that lies before humanity

## I. Universal destiny of every religion

If we searched deeply we should find an 'overlapping consensus' on the truth that all religions belong to the entire human race, and no religion is in possession of the immediate community of its believers. From a Christian perspective we could reflect on these foundations. The narratives of the Fall in the Genesis account (Gen. 3.17–24), the depiction of the times of Noah (Gen. 6.11–13), the construction of the Tower of Babel (Gen. 11.3ff.) – all these refer to the common experience of humankind across nations and races.

'The earth is the Lord's and all that is in it' (Ps. 24.1); so do all religions belong to humankind, under divine dispensation. No religion can claim full ownership of its beliefs and practices. Ownership in the Christian tradition, after all, is justified only when it is for the purpose of *autarkia* and *koinonia* (self-governance and communion).[1] Therefore, belonging to a religion does not close doors; it acquires sense only in so far as it is a means for communion. As for understanding of religions, precisely because they and their scriptures belong to humankind, they are open to a wide spectrum of interpretations. The Indian classical hermeneutical tradition compared texts to a woman and said that the fact that a father has generated a daughter need not mean that he is also the best judge of her beauty; the best judge could be her admirer, lover, or husband. The modern hermeneutical tradition of autonomy of texts could be profitably applied to the religious traditions whose interpretation need not necessarily be confined to the group of believers but is open-ended.

First and foremost, all religions belong to humankind as a whole and *in a primary sense*, while a particular religion belongs to the limited community of its believers in a *secondary and derivative sense*. This is similar to what has been said in Christian tradition on the universal destiny of earthly goods, which takes precedence over the right of private property. In this approach, two things follow: every religion needs to consider itself as addressed to the whole of humanity; consequently, we can all draw on the whole heritage of humanity to the extent that it enhances our life spiritually, and responds to our quest.

Second, the mystery with which all religions are concerned is not the possession of any particular religion. It belongs to the whole human family, which participates in that mystery and manifests its splendour through its life and its varied expressions – including religious ones. Obviously, no religion can claim to exhaust that mystery, much less to possess it. That would be a sin against humankind for having claimed for oneself what, in reality, belongs to all. Moreover, to be believers means to be *witnesses*. Belonging to a religious group does not entitle one to possession of that particular religion, because believing is a witnessing to what one has experienced of the mystery. It follows that what witnesses experience surpasses them and the realm of the community or religious group in which this witnessing takes place.

Third, the various experiences of religions – creeds, rituals, and the like – are not an end in themselves, but only a means. Even scripture is only a means according to St Augustine, who distinguishes between *use* and *enjoyment* – the latter identified with the experience of God.[2] Religion is a penultimate reality and not the ultimate one. It is a means to something greater – and this greater is the mystery that surrounds us all. For the mystery is that which unites all religions and confers meaning and sustenance on them. The experience and enjoyment of the ultimate mystery to which the entire human family is called is nourished with the wide variety of foods the religions offer, and no one has full control of the spiritual metabolism of the experience and enjoyment the mystery brings.

## II. Community of humankind – the mission of all religions

In the post-Westphalian world, nationalism came as a solution to religious conflicts and wars, as it proposed to rise above religious identities. Ironically, what then emerged was nationalism *in the name of religion and religious identities*. Secularism was another effort to contain religions and their nefarious influence. But then it led to the separation of public life and private sphere, with religion relegated to the private domain. In spite of these developments, religion continues to retain its place as a source of moral knowledge and as a system that, though not specialized, may nevertheless respond to questions of momentous significance for humanity – questions not raised in other societal systems or remaining unanswered. One such momentous question is human destiny: its future, its survival, and its unity. This issue needs to be addressed by all religions alike.

Among the religions, there are heated debates on the question of revelation, absoluteness, universality, and so on. There is little discussion, however, on the mission of religions other than one's own in what concerns the crucial question of the destiny of humanity. The converging point of the mission of various religions should be the future shape of the human community and its flourishing. This recognition of the mission of other religions and the awareness of being on a common journey toward a shared future can build up the community of humanity as one single family. Respect for other religions necessarily includes respect for the *mission* to which people of particular religious groups feel called, especially when this mission has something to contribute to the unity of the human family and its flourishing. In this context, the problem of the claim to absoluteness and monopolistic possession of truth is as much a question of the unity and communion of the human community as it is a question of truth and epistemology.

## III. Reverse or incoming universality

If Christianity is to be able to foster the community of humankind it needs to practise reverse universality. Let me explain what that means. In its early days, Christianity allowed its sacred book to be translated into all languages, which is recognition of the universality of the human family. Then, Christianity sent out missionaries to the entire world – again recognition of the universality of humankind. But these two forms of universality are incomplete. Christianity needs to allow itself to be interpreted and reshaped by what these peoples with their cultures and religious traditions have to say about humanity and human destiny. As long as this reverse universality or incoming universality, in contrast to outgoing universality, does not happen, Christianity is only a semi-universal religion, and incomplete. The idea of Christianity as mission spanning the whole of humanity as the recipients of its Good News is a unilateral universality, whereas for Christianity to be more completely universal requires multilateral universality, which calls for the reading and interpretation of its message by diverse peoples through their conceptions of the destiny of the human family. If the outgoing universality is from God; so is the incoming universality for which Christianity needs to make room. It is dogmatism and fostering of stratified Christian identity that make it difficult to accept the incoming universality. The incoming universality is the movement by which the Christian faith is appropriated by humanity as its own.

One way of keeping reverse universality alive is to ask: What does each of those doctrines we hold have to say to humanity at large? This is an important criterion that will save the religions from becoming entangled in internal discussions and getting lost in texts and exegesis. For example, what polygenism or monogenism has to do with humanity is more important than choosing between these two positions for the sake of upholding the authority of the Bible. Upholding polygenism and yet believing in the unity of the

human family is more important than maintaining monogenism and practising racism, as if human beings do not form one single family and as if some
peoples and races are more equal than others. If monogenism can co-exist
with the practice of racism and polygenism with affirmation of the unity of
the whole of human family, this only shows us the urgent need for a self-
critique of religious beliefs – including Christian beliefs – regarding what
they have to contribute to the creation of human community and its
flourishing. The great Thai Buddhist monk Buddhadasa realized this truth
when he said: 'If an interpretation of any word in any religion leads to
disharmony and does not positively further the welfare of the many, then
such an interpretation is to be regarded as wrong; that is against the will of
God, or as the working of Satan or Mara.'[3]

## IV. Religious cosmopolitanism

What I have said about religions belonging to the entire human race and
about reverse universality can be expressed through the concept of religious
cosmopolitanism. While cosmopolitanism is discussed in political and legal
circles, there is little talk of it in connection with religion. One reason for this
may be the impression that religion goes against the spirit of cosmopolitanism. For many, to be cosmopolitan is to sever the links with religion.
Cosmopolitanism is suspicious of religion and the loss of universalistic
perspectives the association with it could entail.

By religious cosmopolitanism is meant the basic attitude, and the attendant mode of practice, that considers all religions the heritage of humanity.
It is a mode of existence in which a person has the ability to enter into the
religious world of the other. It is a deeply human and spiritual attitude. If
political cosmopolitanism is rooted in one's particular nation but at the same
time open to others, so also is religious cosmopolitanism. What religious
cosmopolitanism does is to challenge religious ontology identified with
doctrines, laws, and regulations, just as political cosmopolitanism challenges
national ontology. Religious cosmopolitanism tends to bridge religions as a
communion of communities.

## V. Two senses of cosmopolitanism

There could be a bourgeois theory of cosmopolitanism,[4] at home with
globalization, transnational projects, western classical antiquity,[5] and, not
least, with capitalism. Today, under the capitalistic dispensation, cosmo-

politanism has become the virtue of, so to say, 'frequent travellers', dealing with peoples across cultural and ethnic boundaries, involved in the same mode of production, distribution, and consumption of goods and services. On the other hand, civilizational and humanistic cosmopolitanism is embedded in the particular and in solidarity with the local. The particular could be one's nation, ethnicity, culture, geographic region, language, and so forth, and these are not necessarily in opposition to cosmopolitanism, as is often mistakenly assumed. Cosmopolitan transcendence consists not in setting aside these primordial realities of human groups but in the quest for alternative modes of life along with *other groups, other peoples, and cultures*, thereby challenging the neo-liberal, individualistic cosmopolitanism with its claim to universal reason. This humanistic and community-sensitive cosmopolitanism is not a political theory but a praxis with civilizational roots. It is this kind that also provides the framework for understanding and practising religious cosmopolitanism.

We hear of emperors and rulers through whose support religion thrived. Rarely do we hear of emperors who were inspired by the spirit of religious cosmopolitanism and co-existence. Among these are the Indian emperors Ashoka (304–232 B.C.) and Akbar (1542–1605 A.D.).[6] They represent a counter-paradigm to the *cujus regio eius religio* (religion of the ruler – the religion of the region). Though a Buddhist, Ashoka's breadth of vision was such that in one of his edicts he made known that in harming another religion anyone would be harming one's own. This is the same spirit that inspired Akbar, who fostered closer contacts with Christians and Hindus.[7]

Cosmopolitanism needs to be sustained by *solidarity* since the contribution of religions to the future of humanity and its destiny will depend on the extent to which they are able to instil, promote, and sustain mutual obligations. Bereft of solidarity, cosmopolitanism will turn out to be contemplative pluralism that marvels at the plurality of cultures, ethnicity, and so on, but with little of enriching interaction. In cosmopolitanism imbued with the spirit of solidarity, there is a sense of mutual obligation which is not found in contemplative pluralism or in indiscriminate syncretism and hybridism.

## VI. Cosmopolitanism – rootedness *versus* detachment

Cosmopolitanism involves a dialectic of identity and transcendence. This could be expressed in the form of two metaphors – *root* and *journey*. To live is to strike roots; it is equally true that all life is a journey. These two metaphors seem to contradict each other. But very often the most sublime truths irrupt on to our horizons in the form of contradictions. One such contradiction is human existence, which is rooted, situated, circumscribed, and yet it is a journey. Both the predictable and the unpredictable meet and merge in the stream of life. Our religious experience and belonging show this basic character of the human condition. To create an enclave in which to shore up one's identity is to insulate oneself from the stream of life of others, and this is as undesirable as the dissolution of identities in the waters of misconceived cosmopolitanism.

For most people, when it comes to religion, it appears but natural to be rooted in one's religion and its tradition. But it rarely occurs to believers that one needs to be at the same time detached from one's religion. Religious cosmopolitanism precisely takes place in this dialectic between rootedness and detachment. Viewed from this perspective, religious cosmopolitanism would be the attempt to construct a collective non-tribal self of a particular religious group. Christianity, like other religions, also has its place of roots and times of journey. To the extent that a religious tradition is able to maintain this tension between rootedness and journey, it will be in a position to commune and share itself with other religious traditions and experiences. Religious cosmopolitanism is a way of life that opens up to the riches of the experience of the other as well as its distinctness, while refusing to take the short-cut of hybridism.

## VII. Condition for the creation of community

If there are no common threads among religions and no strands of convergence, if religions exist in a scattered way with no continuity among themselves, there is little likelihood of creating true communities. Religious postures claiming discontinuity with other religions disrupt the important goal of creating community to which all religions are called. If Christians and Christian leaders take offence in praying together with peoples of other faiths (as happened after Pope John Paul II's encounter in Assisi with leaders of other faiths), what kind of community can we expect to foster?. This can only discredit Christian efforts for the creation of community. The contribution by Christianity to the creation of communities can supplement political efforts and other initiatives towards the creation of community, so urgently needed. The importance of this role is brought out by Stanley Samartha when he observes: 'The Church is in danger of being considered as the debris left behind by the receding tide of colonialism, if in its fears of syncretism, it tends to keep itself separate from the neighbours. The problem for India is how, in a multi-religious, multi-lingual, multi-ethnic society, true community life can be fostered so that the nation can move forward. In Pakistan and Sri Lanka, in Malaysia and Indonesia, the problems are the same.'[8]

Syncretism does not produce martyrs, but religious identities do. Now the challenge for the various religious traditions is whether their openness to humanity and its futures is such that they can generate witnesses and martyrs who will uphold that harmony of which syncretism is but a poor specimen. On the other hand, claims of absolutism and monopoly of truth divide the human community and diminish the prospects of the unity of the human family to which all religions declare themselves to be committed.

## VIII. Threats to community: single identity and selective rationality

In the light of what I have said, it makes sense to state that religions do not belong to a particular community, but belong to the whole of humankind. This could serve as a safeguard against the polarization of religion based precisely on a reduction of identity to that of one's religion. One of the root causes of violence and terror at the global level is precisely the reduction of the complex and multi-layered identities of people into simplified religious identity and labels. This is not at all helpful for the unity of the human community.

Viewing people solely from their religious affiliation not only distorts the reality of multiple identities of a person, but also ignores the fact that the same religious tradition is lived in a variety of ways depending upon different geographic, social, cultural, and historical configurations. Further, reading history or interpreting history through religious identity could eclipse the interplay of social, economic, and cultural factors that have been at work in the making of history. For example, when Mahmud of Ghazni (979–1030 A.D.) made fourteen incursions into India, he plundered Hindu temples including the marvellous Somnath temple (in 1024). This he did not because the places of worship were *Hindu*, but because they were fabulously rich with gold, diamonds, and other precious jewels.

Traditionally the claim of superiority for one's religion on the basis of its faith, its privileged revelation, scriptures, and the like was a major source of conflict with other traditions. Today, there is a new threat to inter-religious understanding and world peace when rationality is claimed for one's own religion, while other religions are viewed as irrational or wanting in rationality. Such a mindset makes us wonder with the Indian poet Tagore whether 'the clear stream of reason has not lost its way into the dreary desert sand of dead habits'[9]. 'Dead habits' and tradition can quite often pass for rationality and fuel dangerous confrontation with other religious traditions.

## Conclusion

No single religion can determine humanity's destiny – the destiny of humankind and its unity. All religions have their role in saving the human race, which is done credibly when they do it jointly. For this to happen we need to cultivate religious cosmopolitanism and reverse universality. Inter-religious dialogue is an inadequate category and means. Hence, there is a need to shift towards the concept and practice of religious cosmopolitanism. The point of reference in inter-religious dialogue is religious ontologies – doctrinal tenets, symbolic codes, ethical injunctions, ritual practices, and so forth. In religious cosmopolitanism, on the other hand, the point of reference is the *other*, the source of reverse or incoming universality. The difference the other constitutes is not adequately responded to by a mere aesthetic pluralism that endorses diversity, but by a cosmopolitanism that is sustained by the spirit of solidarity and translated into corresponding practice.

Religious cosmopolitanism is very often practised most effectively at the grassroots level and in very local circumstances. For religious cosmopolitanism cuts across opposition between global and local. Its scope and moral concern are not coterminous with one's particular religious affiliation, as they expand to embrace the whole of humanity. A person may be exposed to the diversity of the various religious universes and yet be chauvinistic and narrow, bent in on his or her limited religious community. On the other hand, at the level of local traditions in small places there could be true cosmopolitan religious practice and mode of life.

The spirit of religious cosmopolitanism will assist in exploding the historically untenable myth that some religious traditions are rational while others are not – a position that has now posed a new threat to world peace and understanding among the various religious traditions. Religious cosmopolitanism does not permit any singular overarching understanding of the universal and the rational but rather invites us to mutual obligation and to engaging the other in the practice of religion – obligations and engagements that have a new dawn for humankind as their hope.

## Notes

1. Cf. Charles Avila, *Ownership. Early Christian Teaching*, Maryknoll, NY: Orbis, 1983.
2. Cf. Jeanrond Werner, *Theological Hermeneutics. Development and Significance*, , New York: Crossroad, 1991, pp. 22–3.
3. As quoted in Kari Storstein Haug, 'Christianity as a Religion of Wisdom and Karma: A Thai Buddhist Interpretation of Selected Passages from the Gospels', in The Council of Societies for the Study of Religion, *Bulletin*, vol. 35, no. 2 (April 2006), p. 43.
4. Today in political theory one speaks of trans-national world-citizenship, drawing inspiration from Kant's theory of cosmopolitan right, something that has been reconstructed with new impetus and radicalness in the work of Jürgen Habermas. Such theoretical exercises may confer legitimacy on the trans-national European Union, but to what extent they are applicable to other parts of the world remains a serious question.
5. Martha Nussbaum and others have developed political cosmopolitanism deriving inspiration from western classical antiquity. We are reminded of Diogenes ('I am a citizen of the world'). See Martha Nussbaum and Joshua Cohen, *For Love of Country. Debating the Limits of Patriotism*, Boston: Beacon Press, 1996. To this heritage we need to add also the cosmopolitan milieux created by the Islamic civilization in Córdoba and Granada during the eighth to the fifteenth centuries, in Egypt and in the Ottoman Empire. Under the Islamic cosmopolitanism there thrived such great thinkers as Ibn Rushd (Averroes) showing the West the way to the riches of western classical antiquity. The cosmopolitan cultural effervescence favoured the emergence of such inter-cultural thinkers as Maimonides in the thirteenth century.
6. A report of the period tells how Akbar was truly a religious cosmopolitan and had regular dialogue and discussion with different religious groups, including Christian missionaries. 'And later that day the emperor came to Fathpur. There he used to spend much time in the Hall of Worship in the company of learned men and sheikhs . . . when he would sit up there the whole night continually occupied in discussing questions of religion, whether fundamental or collateral. . . . Learned monks also from Europe, who are called *Padre,* and have an infallible head, called *Papa* . . . brought the Gospel, and advanced proofs for the Trinity. His majesty firmly believed in the truth of the Christian religion, and wishing to spread the doctrines of Jesus ordered Prince Murad to take a few lessons in Christianity under good auspices, and charged Abul Fazl to translate the Gospel' (W. M. Theodore de Bary *et al.*, eds, *Sources of Indian Tradition*, Delhi: Motilal Banarsidass, 1988, pp. 39–41.
7. Cf. Amartya Sen, *Identity and Violence. The Illusion of Destiny*, London: Penguin Books, 2006, p. 64.

8. Stanley Samartha, *Courage to Dialogue. Ecumenical Issues in Inter-religious Relationship*, Geneva: WCC, 1981, p. 27.
9. Rabindranath Tagore, *Gitanjali*, New York: Macmillan & Co, 1913, poem 35.

# Spirituality and Religious Pluralism

PEDRO CASALDÁLIGA AND JOSÉ MARÍA VIGIL

Theoretically, at least, we have moved beyond those archaic dichotomies: body and soul, spirit and matter, spirituality and action. There is virtually unanimous acceptance that our spirituality is the deep meaning of our life, the major concern of our existence. We believe that spirituality is the true life of each one of us. I am my spirituality. In our book *The Spirituality of Liberation*,[1] especially in the Introduction, we have distinguished this deep dimension of spirituality among various dimensions essential for the spirituality of liberation. The option for the poor is as essential as prayer, solidarity as ecology, militancy as mysticism. All such dimensions make up spirituality lived integrally.

Liberation theology has rediscovered and taken on aspects that in its early stages were not stressed: the dimensions of gender, of culture, of emergent subjects (indigenous peoples, Afro-American peoples). Lately a new factor – and even paradigm – has come to challenge liberation theology and, logically, liberating spirituality: religious pluralism. The plurality of religions can only be seen as a reality that affects us vitally. We have to live together with substantial differences. It is no longer a matter of dialogue on intellectual and doctrinal matters, about peaceful co-existence. We are all involved in constructing the possibility of human beings living in a genuinely shared society with a religious dimension. (Agnosticism and even atheism are also religious options.)

Pluralism, recently discovered, with all its challenges and with no possibility of avoiding it through ignorance, brings a new commitment to religion, theology, and spirituality. Fortunately, theology is already trying to re-draft its concepts in a plural sense.[2] The series '*Por los muchos caminos de Dios*'[3] (Down God's many paths) highlights the 'challenge of religious pluralism to liberation theology', giving some early responses and seeking to work out an initial synthesis of what would be a 'pluralist Latin American liberation theology' and a 'liberating intercontinental theology of religious pluralism'.

What demands are made on spirituality, specifically, by these challenges? What new mode of living spirituality is called for, conjoining the diverse identities within a real and adopted religious pluralism?

Some people will find it easy to dub our proposal 'syncretism'. . . . In the first place, we should accept that there is a syncretism that is not bad. In fact all religions incorporate syncretism, both in their symbolism and in some practices, particularly in areas where there is most popular piety. Furthermore, we have always insisted on open expression of one's own identity. Those who are not religious in any way, or are so in a vague form, with no personal definition, will find it difficult to carry on a serious dialogue, accepting and making valid contributions. We can and should say: 'I am my religious identity'.

Religion, like culture (of which religion is the soul), is dynamic, ongoing, historical. (Despite its institutional, perhaps petrified, structures.) Every institution tends, out of self-defence, to stability, to centralism, to control; religious institutions are no exception.

Faced with all these challenges, we make some suggestions here, confident that we are all increasingly people who want to live our spirituality with a pluralist approach. These suggestions could, we believe, become essential markers and paths.

Living and promoting pluralist spirituality is not just one more fashion, one more activity that we can well do without. We see it as something fundamental to the make-up of a true, integral spirituality at the present time. 'Furthermore, before and beneath the theology of religious pluralism comes the spirituality of religious pluralism, which breathes and spreads even without books and theologies: as if by osmosis, by intuition, as a work of the Spirit, "down God's many paths"'.[4]

## I. Confessional humility

For centuries we have lived our Christian faith, defending it and propagating it, at times, in certain periods, with a spirit of self-sufficiency, of dogmatism, and of proselytism. At most, we may, at certain times, have taken part in an ecumenical and even a macro-ecumenical act, but all the while basically believing that we possessed the fullness of truth and carrying out these gestures, perhaps, out of courteous condescension. We did not do so believing this was both fruit and demand of the Spirit.

Apart from theological discussions and some outbursts of violence – often even physical – in day-to-day life we were generally tolerant. But we did not carry our spirituality with the explicit consciousness of accepting it as one spirituality among many. At the risk of caricature, we might say that, in practice, we behaved as though our spirituality were not only the best, but the only valid one. We came to proclaim, through our lives, that outside the Christian Church there was no spirituality, just as we came to declare that outside the Church there was no salvation. Our spirituality and the holiness of our saints were supernatural; the virtues of non-Christians were natural virtues, mere ethics.

If we are to practise the confessional humility we are suggesting, we shall evidently have to move beyond prejudices, broaden our religious outlook, learn how to receive enriching contributions from all religions.[5] Saying 'humility' has nothing to do with an inferiority complex; on the contrary, we believe that spirituality, any spirituality, and in this case Christian spirituality, should be lived in an adult, free, co-responsible manner. Only if we live our own spirituality with lucidity shall we be able to able to dialogue and share with other spiritualities.

Confessional humility accords with the new universal situation of scientific humility, of epistemological humility. Faith – and now we accept this, even if only from necessity – is not evidence. Uncertainty, and even doubt, form part of religion. All true religion is a quest, as passionate as it is humble. We believe but do not see. God continues his revelation to us in the midst of our personal and collective vicissitudes. We do not defend our faith with crusades and anathemas. We live it in gratitude and we want to share it gratuitously, respecting and welcoming other faiths.

## III. Spiritual openness

That self-sufficient posture we referred to is both the root and the fruit of distancing ourselves, consciously or not. As still happens in certain more fundamentalist communities, we used to avoid even contact with people of other confessions. There is still a long road to travel to make reparation for religious violence and to purify ourselves, in mind and heart, in our spirituality.

A first step is being prepared to learn, to distinguish, to relativize. A second step is reading, studying. A third step is involvement in, jointly taking up major challenges, human causes that, for us as believers in the God of Life, are divine causes. It has often been said recently that there will be peace in the world only if there is peace among the religions, and that there will be peace among the religions only if they talk to one another. Inter-religious dialogue (ecumenical and macro-ecumenical) is spirituality. And it will increasingly be so if we can experience globalization, that inevitable and at the same time providential challenge, spiritually.

This spiritual openness is demanding both in the amount of past it has to move beyond and in all it has to take on in our growing and accelerating global village. The world belongs to all and is for all, and the religious aspect of the world also belongs to all and is for all. It is no good drifting through life with a Missal in hand or a Bible under one's arm. The Bible, the Missal, and the Koran . . . are religious mediations in the service of God's Kingdom or Project for humankind and the universe. The Churches are becoming more sensitive to Jesus' witness ('that they may all be one'; John 17.21), but they have to become ever more sensitive to the urgency of this unity, not only for Christians but for the whole of humankind.

## IV. Commitment in solidarity

Spirituality, we said, is one's own personal life, in depth, which must be, always, at the same time a life lived in community. We shall live pluralism if we act in solidarity with all the 'living forces' promoting solidarity, in those great causes that we Christians define as the kingdom of God.

We plead for a spirituality that is pluralist and liberating. Our starting point is the spirituality of liberation. We believe the great features of this spirituality should be lived in a pluralism that is truly human and humaniz-ing. The spirituality of liberation was, initially, Latin American. Communi-ties, movements, meetings, congresses, theologians . . . have been extending this spirituality and enriching it with very specific contributions from other continents. As a result, liberating praxis is becoming ever more a pluralist, inter-religious praxis. God has become greater, being no longer 'my God', our God'; God is God, the God of all names, and is, always, the God of the poor, the God who hears the cry of the oppressed and comes down to set them free.

Mercy, which is characteristic of Jesus' God, is becoming ever more sensitive to suffering and struggle in all parts of the globe. From where we happen to be, we embrace the world, spiritually. 'Do not do your neighbour the harm you would not wish for yourself, and do to your neighbour the good you would wish for yourself': all religions have promulgated this as their first maxim. Religious spirituality is solidarity; it is effective; it is the love that can pass even the toughest test Jesus proposed. It lives by giving life and gives its own life if the hour comes. The martyrs are the best witnesses to a pluralist liberating spirituality. Martyr blood is universal, flowing over all frontiers.

The spirituality we dream of is the practice of Justice, of Love-Justice. The option for the poor is not just one among so many characteristics of true spirituality; it is an essential option, which makes the difference and judges religious truth and practice. 'Truth, Pilate, means placing oneself on the side of the poor.'[6] If there are spiritualities that give first place to the silence of contemplation, or ecological wonderment, we recognize the option for the poor, in mercy, justice, and love as the religious *analogatum princeps*. The ideal, clearly, is a holistic spirituality, one that embraces all these dimensions, in plurality and in complementarity. Better 'the difficult whole' than 'the better part'.[7]

## V. Daily practice

In daily practice we shall live this spirituality by:

- making explicit space for the other religions in our daily prayer and liturgical celebrations;
- regularly reading and studying the history of these religions, their sacred texts, and the spiritualities that characterize each of them;
- taking part in macro-ecumenical courses, meetings, and celebrations, as well as promoting new platforms for inter-religious encounter, for theology, spirituality, and pastoral work (and their equivalents in each religious tradition);
- not allowing other religious practices to be undervalued in our circles and avoiding dismissive expressions, signs, and actions;
- introducing, in our respective Churches, the respected and loved presence of that plural God, greater, universal, of all names, and of no name exclusively, and showing that God is always the God of Love, of Hope, and of Peace.

Making room for accepting religious pluralism does not dispense us from religious self-criticism or criticism. We must always take care that God's name is not blasphemed on our account. We need to shoulder the mission of helping our communities to overcome fundamentalisms, exclusivities, superstitions, and interpretations that are unworthy of the present time. True pluralist religion has to be free and freeing. The deepest slavery, as it is the most radical, is religious slavery.

*Translated by Paul Burns*

*Notes*

1. P. Casaldáliga and J. M. Vigil, *Espiritualidad de la liberación*, Quito: Verbo Divino, 1992, ch. 1. (Eng. trans. *The Spirituality of Liberation*, Tunbridge Wells: Burns & Oates; Marknoll, NY: Orbis, 1994.)
2. A similar approach is essayed in J. M. Vigil, *Teología del pluralismo religioso. Curso sistemático de teología popular*, Córdoba, Spain: El Almendro; Quito, Ecuador: Abya Yala, 2005.
3. Cf. ASETT, 'Por los muchos caminos de Dios' series, 5 vols., Quito: Abya Yala, 2002 –; available at latinoamericana.org/tiempoaxial.
4. J. M. Vigil, L. Tomita, and M. Barros, *Por los muchos caminos de Dios. Teología liberadora intercontinental del pluralismo religioso*, Quito: Abya Yala, 2006.
5. There is more religious truth in all the religions as a whole than in any single religion, and this is true also of Christianity: E. Schillebeeckx, *Church, the Human Story of God*, London: SCM; New York: Crossroad, 1990 (here Port. ed., p. 215). 'There is more "religious" truth in the sum of all religions than in any religion on its own, including Christianity itself': C. Geffré, 'O lugar das religiões no plano da Salvação', in F. Teixeira (ed.), *O diálogo inter-religiosos como afirmação da vida*, São Paulo: Paulus, 1997, p. 121.
6. 'A passage by Van der Meersch marked my understanding of the intellectual endeavour: "'Truth, Pilate, is this: placing oneself on the side of the little ones and those who suffer." This passage helped me to understand that truth requires taking the side of the poor, of the oppressed, of those who are being persecuted; in short, that the service of truth requires self-commitment alongside them; these are the historical dimensions of truth: placing oneself on the side of the little ones and those who suffer, not defending truth from an office, but in a way that can commit one on the side of those who are suffering the injustices.' Alfonso Comín in *Misión Abierta* 70 (Mar. 1977), back cover.
7. P. Casaldáliga, 'El difícil todo', in *Antología mariana*, Madrid, Claretianas, 1991, p. 76. Available at servicioskoinonia.org/pedro/poesia.
8. H. Küng, *Spurensuche: die Weltreligionen auf dem Weg*, vol. 1, Munich: Piper, 1999. (Eng. trans. *Tracing the Way: Spiritual Dimensions of the World Religions*, London & New York, Continuum, 2002.)

# Conclusion
## Reflecting on the Course: a Clamour and a Light from All Sides

LUIZ CARLOS SUSIN

At the end of this course in different voices, we are in a position to underline the characteristic and recurring accents that pervade the contributors' texts, besides drawing attention to some novelties that they invite us to take further.

In the first place, still using negative terms, the paradigmatic leap is neither a luxury nor a passing fashion. The path taken by the religions till now, without having recourse here to the function of religion in evolutionary theory, can be understood theologically within the economy of salvation and revelation contextualized in a pivotal time that is now drawing to a close and turning into an era when the 'great religions', well adapted to their basically agrarian context, and as they have been lived and constituted up till now, are tending to become sclerotic. The claim or hypothesis of the 'end of religions' clearly arouses a heated debate, since there are arguments – equally debatable – that point to a 'return to religion'. Whether we consider the five centuries of westernizing modernity or extend the consideration to cover the twenty-five centuries of the formation and triumph of the West alongside the prophetic reform of the Middle East or the Buddhist reform in Asia, the present-day map is one of pivotal 'great transformation' of the age, which impacts strongly on the forms taken by religion. Leonardo Boff even prefers to examine the current transformation from the temporal perspective of the universe and life on Planet Earth.

Christianity, which at first stood out for its 'modernity', for its humility and creative adaptability, in the shadow of its eschatological nature, nevertheless carries, as it journeys towards the future, the tragic weight of its conquering, colonizing, devastating, death-dealing expansion, which today threatens the entirety of life on earth. The 'Constantinian tack', gradually turning Christianity into a religion of empire, marks the whole later course of the Christian adventure. Humankind would undoubtedly be poorer without Christianity, and Christian values continue to provide a golden thread and a resource that delighted, for example, Gandhi and Tagore. But the ambiguity implicit in its mission, as Tissa Balasuriya states here from Sri Lanka, forces Christianity to rethink itself in relation to other traditions and forms of religion. Its finest contribution at present would be to help produce the attitudes required for a just recognition of the settings of multiform divine revelation and salvation, an urgent dialogue demanded by the 'other' peoples of 'other' religions, who – and not by coincidence – are the poor peoples of the earth. This, then, would be a dialogue among the various religious traditions, with the respect and credibility dialogue supposes, starting from the traditions of the poor peoples of the earth. Academic theology will be fruitful to the extent that it listens to and seeks to be faithful to the religious experience of the poor peoples and their witness.

We are in a position clearly to understand that religious pluralism does not come about through imperfection; neither should it be accepted with a mere gesture of tolerance. We are still weighed down by the Hellenic reasoning that 'multiplicity' is degradation and defect, while *unum est totum*. On the other hand, the ancient Guaraní people, from the heart of Lain America, challenge us with, 'We are under the *one*, and that is bad'. Left to themselves, peoples love plurality as they love colours. Such plurality starts from God's creative design, which loves variety and creates fruitful biodiversity. It is in the logic of divine creation, which cloning and uniformity abhor, that we understand theologically the leap towards the biodiversity and growing complexity that make the universe a wonder.

Human biodiversity, however, symbolized by languages and cultures, is beginning to depend also on our decisions and our creation. It can turn into violence and confusion, but this is neither the original intention nor the last word on diversity read theologically. The religious traditions, powerful through being sacred, belong in this logical line. There is a religious pluralism 'on principle', stressed here by Faustino Teixeira. Unity is realized not in uniformity but in the coming together and communion that reach their depth in mysticism – *Deus intimior et superior religione mea* – and in which God is praised and served in the 'religion pure and undefiled' that, according to James, 'is this: to care for orphans and widows in their distress, and to keep oneself unstained by the world' (Jas 1.27).

There is an implicit and recurring, always unavoidable, question lying at the origin of any thinking about religion, just as in philosophy one always asks what philosophy is: What, ultimately, is religion itself? The sciences, history, anthropology, literature, psychoanalysis, even market interests, all bend over backwards seeking to unravel the meaning of religion. On the level of human culture, it represents the 'soul' of a culture, as the 'Dialogue and Proclamation' issued by the Pontifical Council for Inter-religious Dialogue states in its section 45, or 'the heart of the culture', as Andrés Torres Queiruga reminds us here, quoting Benedict XVI. As we must do justice to the plurality of cultures, then we need to speak of 'hearts', in the plural. Marcelo Barros and the ASETT team suggest using the neologism 'hiero-diversity' to describe this 'sacred diversity' of the hearts of cultures within cultural biodiversity. Communion in a *perichoresis* of hearts becomes possible if there is contemplation of 'the sacred of the other' and heart-to-heart hospitality; this involves both trial and risk, as Barros, a monk living among Afro-Brazilian cults, points out, following the path of Christian mystics who have immersed themselves deeply in Hindu, Buddhist, and indigenous traditions. It is true that we may neither confuse religion with nor separate it from revelation and salvation. Religions are ways of revelation and of salvation, symbolic ways that can even turn diabolical, just as icons can turn into idols. Or, using other metaphors, they are wells that help us to reach the source, landscapes with many paths and many sources, as Paulo Suess makes clear from his experience among the multiplicity of indigenous peoples in Brazil: they need to be providers of paths.

Every time religions, especially the most widespread missionary ones, make use of the classical category of *election*, they actually close off paths and practise persecution of the other, exclusion, and condemnation. Emanuel Levinas interpreted 'election' positively as *responsibility*, an experience of uniqueness and of irreplaceableness in the virtually maternal relationship with others. Somewhat like St Bernard's exclamation: *quia amati, amamus!* This is a category synonymous with messianism, *anointing*. The writers in this issue would place us on guard against the historical and diabolical excesses and the permanent danger of messianism, of Christianity *tout court* that is. Christ and Christians, with their mission and *raison d'être* in the world, together with Islam, are at the heart of this question, to which I shall return later.

Andrés Torres Queiruga has recourse here to the neologism *inreligiona-tion*, a much deeper and more delicate step than *inculturation*. This is because inreligionation is related to the heart of a culture and heart-to-heart reception! It is more challenging because it is more specific than inculturation, even though it is inseparable from the dialogue among cultures in which hearts beat and give life. In this sense, language especially but also icons, narrative, rites, canons, dogma, all open paths and cultural symbols are also an invitation to move beyond them in the same way that we serve them and savour them. The necessity for considering language as Javier Melloni, José Amando Robles, and Lieve Troch do here, taking epistemology and its limits seriously, particularly the trying-out of new images, is an urgent one in our times. We need a current deconstruction within a permanent deconstruction if fundamentalism is not to make religion an all-powerful arm capable of bringing about the chaos we are presently witnessing. In epistemological terms, the editors suggested to Robles that he might delve into the statement that each religion is a map of but not the actual territory of salvation. He carries the metaphor further, comparing religious knowledge to artistic knowledge, but still more radical: it leads to the experience that surpasses all objective knowledge, experience of the first being last – 'bottomless and formless', that is, without even a map. Art savours form, while religious knowledge, being of an etymologically 'metaphorical' order, overflows into the purest mysticism, in the Presence that is Mystery.

What, then, is left for us, pilgrims in the Mystery, who need language and forms of religion? 'Religious cosmopolitanism', the attitude that affirms what is local, regional, and global, what belongs to us and what belongs to others, always in an open manner, can help to raise us above narcissism and elitism. So Felix Wilfred invites us to adopt a correct posture of welcoming religious traditions: religions, with their riches and resources, belong to the whole of humanity; they are an inheritance and patrimony of the entire human race, and only secondarily does each religion have a relationship of belonging with its specific believers. *There is a universal destiny for each form of religion*. The metaphor of the relationship of the common good to private property and its priority over this is very pertinent. While no one form of religion exhausts the mystery, on the other hand the value of each form lies in its fruits of communion and unity within humanity and in the future of humanity that it promotes. There is, therefore, no better society that would have a privileged destiny to universality. As in the organization of life and society, so also in encounters among religious traditions, the principles of both *autarkia* and *koinonia* hold good.

Finally, missionary traditions, of which Christianity and Islam are perhaps the main examples, also need to make the paradigmatic leap. 'Religious mission' in the world is formed by, begins with, lasts in, and is fulfilled in 'dialogue', the language of religious metaphors but most importantly of *interlocutors*. Now, dialogue and interlocutors suppose pluralism, and pluralism stimulates and revivifies mission as dialogue. There is, however, a lot of mission, as Paul Knitter humorously observes, without losing sight of the extreme seriousness of dialogue and 'mutuality', an operational, methodological form of communion. Dialogical mutuality also contains proclamation and speech, but accompanied by listening, apprenticeship, and acceptance. The relationship between master and pupil is not one-way but is carried on in mutuality. Mission is, metaphorically, like water, in which oxygen and hydrogen need each other for it to exist – in this case, hearing and saying. The mutual offering helps in the 'reversal' of mission, as apprenticeship in relation to the precious originality of the other: in the end, others as such have in themselves more content than all the content they can offer, So religious traditions are not treated as 'all equal' but as the precise opposite, as 'all original' and different, which in effect turns the risk of change into an opportunity for enrichment and vitality. The greatest challenge to encounter and dialogue among religious traditions has always been and still is between East and West. In recent centuries, however, history has forced the emergence of a North–South dialogue, and recently that between Christianity and Islam has become urgent from various points of view.

Christianity in particular has not been stripped of universalism and of its unrenounceable messianism – a double assertion needed to clarify its essence: Christianity is the confession of Jesus as Messiah, Christ offered to all. Now, anyone 'doctored in Christianity' well knows that, in Christian experience, the Christ 'Jesus' is an 'off-centre Christocentrism', as Claude Geffré insisted some time ago. Perhaps, despite the venerable tradition regarding 'Christocentrism' derived, in the New Testament, primarily from John and Paul, backed up by the Hellenic language of the early councils, it would be more appropriate now, in this time of paradigmatic shift, to use the metaphor of 'the way', an obviously *non-narcissistic* way: those who reach the heart of Jesus as Christ come to a stripped heart and to a crossroads with many paths: to the Father in his reserve of Mystery, to the Spirit in its impulse to incarnation together with others, to 'the least' in their flesh and blood, and finally to 'others' in their cultural and religious otherness. Even to the stars, to the cosmos, that great horizon of creation and eschatology in the Christian tradition of the cosmic Christ, as Leonardo Boff stresses.

José María Vigil emphasizes the main Christian difficulty, the *punctum dolens* that is not so much church-centredness or exclusiveness, largely left behind by Vatican II, but Christocentric inclusiveness: how to change our perception of Jesus as Christ on the basis of the emerging pluralist paradigm. He points out that the problem is not Jesus as he is presented in the New

Testament, but the later dogma developed in the fourth and fifth centuries, which for generations in the Early Middle Ages provided the answer to the question, 'And you? Who do you say that I am?' Our generation, living in a different world, freed now from the duties of a 'religion of empire', with a different understanding of revelation and an experience of religious pluralism never previously known, has the right and indeed the obligation to give its own answer to the question, an answer stripped, for the first time, of a superiority complex toward those other brothers and sisters who walk 'down God's many paths'. Christianity is called to a cosmopolitanism in which there is acceptance, hospitality, offering, in which *Gloria Dei homen [pauper] vivens, Gloria coelorum terra vivens.*

*Translated by Paul Burns*

# Contributors

JOSÉ AMANDO ROBLES is a Spanish Dominican and a naturalized citizen of Costa Rica. He holds a doctorate in sociology from Louvain (1991) and his main field of study is religion in knowledge-based societies. He teaches at the Ecumenical School of Religious Studies at the National University of Costa Rica and manages the Meister Eckhart Programme for the Dominican Research Centre in Heredia. His publications include *La religión, de la Conquista a la Modernidad* (1992), *Repensar la religión. De la creencia al conocimiento* (2001), and *Hombre y mujer de conocimiento. La propuesta de Juan Matus y Carlos Castaneda* (2006).

Address: Apdo. 237, 3000 Heredia, Costa Rica, Central America
E-mail: jarobles@pop-rasca.co.cr

TISSA BALASURIYA was born in 1924 and is a member of the Congregation of Oblates of Mary Immaculate. He studied theology in Rome and politics and economics at Oxford. In 1971 he founded the NGO called CSR (Centre for Society and Religion) in Colombo, Sri Lanka, which has been of great importance on the international scene. He was one of the founders of EAT-WOT/ASSET and has written hundreds of articles and many books on the themes of justice, peace, global theology, and inter-religious dialogue. He is known world-wide for his work with NGOs and international theological associations. Titles published in English include *The Eucharist and Human Liberation* (1979), *Planetary Theology* (1984), *Mary and Human Liberation* (1994), *Globalization and Human Solidarity* (2000).

Address; CSR, 281 Deans Road, Colombo, Sri Lanka
E-mail: tissabalasuriya@hotmail.com

MARCELO BARROS is a Benedictine monk and biblicist, born in 1945. He is a member of the theological commission of EATWOT and adviser to the

Brazilian 'Pastoral Strategy of the Land' commission and to the base church communities. He worked on theology of the land, as an integral part of liberation theology, in the 1980s. At present he lives within a community of African origin and studies cultural and religious pluralism from this standpoint. The author of more than thirty books, his most recent publication is *Dom Helder Câmara, profeta para nossos dias* (2006), already translated into French, Italian, and Dutch.

Address: Avenida dos Ipês, Quadra 53, lote 11, Parque das Laranjeiras, 7488-390 Goiânia – GO, Brazil
e-mail: irmarcelobarros@uol.com.br

LEONARDO BOFF was born in Concórdia in the state of Sanata Catarina in Brazil in 1938 and holds doctorates in theology and philosophy from Munich University (1970). He is Professor Emeritus of ethics and philosophy of religion at the State University of Rio de Janeiro. He is the author of over seventy books, many of which have been translated into English, including *Jesus Christ Liberator* (1978), *Church: Charism and Power* (1985; which led to his famous 'colloquy' with the then Cardinal Ratzinger), *Trinity and Society* (1988), *Ecology and Liberation: A New Paradigm* (1995), *Cry of the Earth, Cry of the Poor* (1997), *Fundamentalism, Terrorism, and the Future of Humanity* (2006).

Address: CP 92144 / 25741-970, Petrópolis, RJ, Brazil.
E-mail: lboff@leonardoboff.com.

PEDRO CASALDÁLIGA PLA was born on 16 February 1928 at Balsareny in Catalonia and is a religious of the Congregation of Claretian Missionaries. He was ordained priest at Montjuich in Barcleona in 1952 and in 1971 consecrated bishop of São Félix do Araguaia, in the Brazilian state of Matto Grosso, where he has lived since 1968. He has been bishop emeritus since 2004. He is a co-founder of CIMI, the Council of Mission to Indigenous Peoples, and of CPT, the Pastoral Land Commission. His campaigns on behalf of the indigenous peoples and the oppressed in general have placed his life in continual danger. A poet and prose writer, he has published many prose and verse works in Spanish, Portuguese, and Catalan, including *Tierra nuestra, libertad* (1974), *Misa de la tierra sin males* (1980), *El tiempo y la espera* (1986), and *Me llamarán subversivo* (1987). Those translated into other languages, including (with J. M. Vigil), *The Spirituality of Liberation* (2004). In

March 2006 he became the first recipient of the 'Catalonia International Prize' awarded by the Catalan Government.

Address: CP 05, Avenida Dr José Fragelli 1310, Vila Nova 78670-000, São Félix do Araguaia/MT, Brazil. Website: www.servicioskoinonia.org/pedro.

PAUL F. KNITTER taught theology at Xavier University in Cincinnati, Ohio, for thirty-one years and has recently assumed the Paul Tillich Chair of Theology, World Religions, and Culture at Union Theological Seminary in New York. He received a licentiate in theology from the Pontifical Gregorian University in Rome (1966) and a doctorate from the University of Marburg, Germany (1972). For the past two decades he has served as editor of Orbis Books' series 'Faith Meets Faith'. From 1986 to 2004 he was on the Board of Directors for CRISPAZ (Cristianos por la Paz en El Salvador), and is presently serving on the Board of Trustees for the International, Inter-religious Peace Council.

Address: Union Theological Seminary, 3041 Broadway at 121st Street, New York, NY 10027, U.S.A.

JAVIER MELLONI is a Jesuit priest and university lecturer. He is a member of 'Christianity and Justice' and lectures in the theology faculty of the university of Catalonia. An anthropologist and doctor of theology, he has published books on the history of religions and is a member of the advisory council of the Parliament of World Religions.

Address: Casa d'Exerciscs 'Cova Sant Ignasi'. C/Cova s/n (Apartat 12), 08240 Manresa (Barcelona), Spain

PAULO SUESS was born in Cologne in 1938 and studied at the universities of Munich, Louvain, and Münster, where he gained a doctorate in Fundamental Theology. He worked in Amazonia for ten years and from 1979 to 1983 he served as general secretary of CIMI, the indigenous pastoral body affiliated to the Brazilian Bishops' National Conference. In 1987 he founded the post-graduate course in Missiology in São Paulo. From 2000 to 2004 he was president of the International Association of Missiology. He is a doctor *honoris causa* of the universities of Bamberg (1993) and Frankfurt (2004). He is currently theological adviser to CIMI. His publications include *Catolicismo Popular no Brasil* (1979), *A Conquista Espiritual da América*

*Espanhola* (1992), *La Nueva Evangelización* (1993), *Travessia com esperança* (²2003).

E-mail: suess@uol.com.br

LUIZ CARLOS SUSIN is professor of systematic theology at the Pontifical Catholic University of Rio Grande do Sul and at the Higher School of Theology and Franciscan Spirituality, both in Porto Alegre, Brazil. He is an ex-president of the Brazilian Society for Theology and Religious Studies, and secretary general of the World Forum for Theology and Liberation. His recent research has been into the relationship between theology and ecology. His publications include *A Criação de Deus* (2003); *Deus, Pai, Filho e Espírito Santo*; *Jesus, Filho de Deus e Filho de Maria*; *Assim na terra como no céu*, some published by Paulinas (São Paulo) and some by Vozes (Petrópolis).

Address: Rua Juarez Tábora 171, 91520-100 Porto Alegre – RS, Brazil
Email: lcsusin@pucrs.br. Website: www.luizcarlossusin.com.

FAUSTINO TEIXEIRA was born in Juiz de Fora in the Matto Grosso province of Brazil in 1954 and is a lay theologian with degrees in philosophy, religious studies, and theology. He holds a doctorate from the Gregorianum in Rome, with a thesis on the base church communities in Brazil, and he returned there in 1997–8 for post-doctoral studies under the guidance of Jacques Dupuis. From 1978 to 1982 and 1986 to 1992 he taught in the theology department of the Pontifical Catholic University of Rio de Janeiro. Since 1989 he has been Professor of Theology of Religions in the post-graduate religious studies programme at the Federal University of Juiz de Fora. He is also a researcher for the National Council for Scientific and Technological Development (CNPQ) and a consultant to the Institute for Religious Studies (ISER-Assessoria). His publications include *A gênese das CEBs no Brasil* (1998); *A espiritualidade de seguimento* (1994); *Teología de las religiones* (2005); *As religiões no Brasil* (2005).

ANDRÉS TORRES QUEIRUGA was born in 1940 in Aguiño-Ribeira in the province of Coruña in Galicia. He holds a doctorate in philosophy and theology and taught fundamental theology from 1968 to 1987. He is currently professor of philosophy of religion at the University of Santiago de Compostela. His publications (most originally in Galician, with title and date of Spanish publication here) include: *La revelación de Dios el la realización del hombre* (1987; also in Ital., Port., Ger., Eng.), *Recuperar la salvación* ($^2$1995), *Creo en Dios Padre* ($^5$1998), *Fin del Cristianismo premoderno* (2000), *Recuperar la creación* ($^3$2001; also in Port.), *Repensar la resurrección* (2003), *Esperanza a pesar del mal* (2005), *Diálogo de las religiones y autoconciencia cristiana* (2005)

Address: Facultade de Filosofía, 15703 Santiago de Compostela, Spain
E-mail: atorres@usc.es

LIEVE TROCH was born in 1949 and is a Belgian national. She lives in the Netherlands, where she teaches systematic theology in the faculty of theology of the Catholic University of Nijmegen. She is also a senior lecturer in the Ecumenical Institute of Religious Science at São Paulo, Brazil, and has been a visiting professor in a number of Asian countries. She has published various articles and is the author of several books in the area of feminist fundamental theology. Her works include: *Verzet is het geheim van de vreugde. Fundamentaaltheologische thema's in een feministische discussie* (Fundamental theological topics in a feminist context; 1996). She is currently working as a feminist theologian carrying out research into the areas of interreligious and intercultural practice.

Address: Min. Nelissenstraat 19, 4818 HS Breda, The Netherlands.
E-mail: l.troch@theo.kun.nl

JOSÉ MARÍA VIGIL was born in Zaragoza in Spain and 're-born' in Managua, Nicaragua. He studied theology in Salamanca and Rome, and psychology in Salamanca, Madrid, and Managua and has taught theology in Salamanca and Managua. He took Nicaraguan citizenship and shared its struggles for thirteen years. He currently works in Panama, and for fifteen years has published, annually, in conjunction with Bishop Pedro Casaldáliga, 'Agenda Latinoamerican' in seven languages and eighteen countries (http://latinomamericana.org). He is theological coordinator of ASETT, responsible for the five-volume 'Por los muchos caminos de Dios', published by Abya Yala in Quito, for whom he also edits the theology series 'Tiempo axial'. His published works also include *Spirituality of Liberation* (also with Casaldáliga; 1994) and *Teología del pluralismo religioso* (2005), besides over 350 articles in theological and pastoral reviews and newspapers.

Address: Apto 0823-03151, Panama City, Panama, C.A.

# *Concilium* Subscription Information

**February**   **2007/1**: *Pluralist Theology*

**April**   **2007/2**: *The Land*

**June**   **2007/3**: *AIDS*

**October**   **2007/4**: *Christianity and Democracy*

**December**   **2007/5**: *Ages of Life and Christian Experience*

*New subscribers*: to receive *Concilium 2007* (five issues) anywhere in the world, please copy this form, complete it in block capitals and send it with your payment to the address below.

- - - - - - - - - - - - - - - - - - - - - - - - - - - - - - - - - - - - - - - - - - - - - - - - - - - - - - - - -

**Please enter my subscription for *Concilium 2007***

Individuals
____ £40.00 UK
____ £60.00 overseas
____ $110.00 North America/Rest of World
____ €99.00 Europe

Institutions
____ £55.00 UK
____ £75.00 overseas
____ $140 North America/Rest of World
____ €125.00 Europe

Postage included – airmail for overseas subscribers

**Payment Details:**
Payment must accompany all orders and can be made by cheque or credit card
I enclose a cheque for £/$/€ _____ Payable to SCM-Canterbury Press Ltd
Please charge my Visa/MasterCard (Delete as appropriate) for £/$/€ _____
Credit card number  ....................................................................................................................
Expiry date  ...............................................................................................................................
Signature of cardholder  .............................................................................................................
Name on card  ...........................................................................................................................
Telephone ................................................ E-mail ...................................................................

**Send your order to *Concilium*, SCM-Canterbury Press Ltd**
9–17 St Albans Place, London N1 ONX, UK
Tel +44 (0)20 7359 8033 Fax +44 (0)20 7359 0049
E-Mail: office@scm-canterburypress.co.uk

**Customer service information:**
*All orders must be prepaid. Subscriptions are entered on an annual basis (i.e. January to December). No refunds on subscriptions will be made after the first issue of the Journal has been despatched. If you have any queries or require information about other payment methods, please contact our Customer Services department.*